Last Full Measure of Devotion

A Tribute to America's Heroes of the Vietnam War

by
Donald J. Farinacci

authorHOUSE®

AuthorHouse™
1663 Liberty Drive, Suite 200
Bloomington, IN 47403
www.authorhouse.com
Phone: 1-800-839-8640

First published by AuthorHouse 10/29/2007

ISBN: 978-1-4343-1857-2 (sc)
ISBN: 978-1-4343-1856-5 (hc)

Library of Congress Control Number: 2007904343

Printed in the United States of America
Bloomington, Indiana

Dedicated to America's Soldiers, Sailors, Airmen and Marines, past and present

"...It is rather for us to be here dedicated to the great task remaining before us, that from these honored dead we take increased devotion to that cause for which they gave the last full measure of devotion..."

Abraham Lincoln
The Gettysburg Address
1863

Table of Contents

Foreword

Forty one years ago, on August 26, 1966, I entered the United States Army. The Vietnam War was raging and hundreds of thousands of American soldiers, sailors and airmen were already "in country". United States forces served in Vietnam from 1961 until 1973 and by the time the last troop transport plane departed that tragic country, 2.7 million Americans had served there. By random chance, fate or providence, I was not one of them. The Army sent me overseas in 1967 but not to Vietnam. My military service is a source of great pride to me and I am grateful for having had the opportunity to serve. But, I fully realize that, not having experienced combat, I cannot possibly comprehend what it is like to know that any second I might simply disappear from the earth forever; and that I will face the same reality tomorrow and for countless days thereafter; nor can I know what effect such transformative knowledge would have on my mind, my body, my world-view and my soul. I cannot answer the question of which is worse, the danger of being killed or the knowledge of having killed.

Nevertheless, I did live through the tumultuous Vietnam era and my memories are vivid, especially of the fellow soldiers I trained with who died in Vietnam. It was a defining experience that has provided me with the passion and emotion to seek to put down on paper a long overdue tribute to those who gallantly served and sacrificed on that distant battle ground.

This is fitting, I believe, because the millions who have fought our wars since 1775 have put themselves at risk so that the rest of us can live in peace and freedom, whether one believes in the rightness of the particular war or not.

This work is not a political tract or polemic. I have left the larger political, philosophical and moral issues to others. I have tried, where possible, however, to interweave what was unique about the Vietnam War with the stories contained in this book.

My principal aim in writing this book was to pay homage to a largely unheralded generation of fighting men and women who, in my opinion, demonstrated a full measure of devotion to their country and each other. Fifty-eight thousand of them died in fulfilling that duty and many hundreds of thousands of others were severely wounded - some permanently crippled in mind, body or spirit. Otto J. Lehrack in his penetrating work, The First Battle, postulates that these losses created a heavy "blood debt" by America to its people. I would take that a step further and submit that the debt is also that of the American people to those who died or were grievously wounded in that cause.

Many books, such as The Greatest Generation, by Tom Brokaw, have extolled the virtues and sung the praises of the valiant and noble generations who fought America's other wars. It is time to pay tribute to America's unsung heroes, its Vietnam warriors; to give them their proper recognition and affirm that what they gave to their country was just as ennobling and worthy of respect as that of any other generation. We owe them no less than that.

America's Vietnam warriors should have been honored by a grateful nation, instead, they were in many cases ignored, cursed, reviled, abused and spit upon.

In my own small way I have tried to make a contribution to righting that wrong, to redressing a grievance rarely voiced by those so aggrieved. I have not waded into the murky ambiguities of America's involvement in Vietnam. It is hard for me to imagine that anything new could be written on that subject. Make no mistake about it - what I have attempted here is an unabashed tribute to our military personnel who fought the Vietnam War and who did so honorably. I have attempted to simply tell some of their stories in as pure a way as possible, free from the taint of the larger moral, political and strategic implications of America's Vietnam experience. It is my fervent hope that their humanity shines through the pages that follow.

I have chosen as the format for this book a series of profiles of Vietnam fighting men. I believe them to be representative of the vast majority of those who fought bravely in Vietnam, and I offer their stories as a tribute to all who risked their lives for the rest of us.

The portraits are in no sense intended as a pantheon of the greatest heroes of Vietnam and, of necessity, many heroes will not be mentioned. It would be an impossible task to relate all or even most tales of Vietnam valor, so the profiles in this book will have to stand for all of them.

Likewise, no slight is intended to the thousands of women who served valiantly in Vietnam, which I hope will be the subject of another book.

Andy Rooney of the CBS television broadcast <u>Sixty Minutes</u>, on May 6, 2001, described a hero as "one who risks his life for his country". This is a book about a generation of heroes.

"Let us have faith that right makes might; and in that faith let us to the end, dare to do our duty as we understand it."
Abraham Lincoln, Cooper Union Speech, 27 February 1860

Indochina 1965

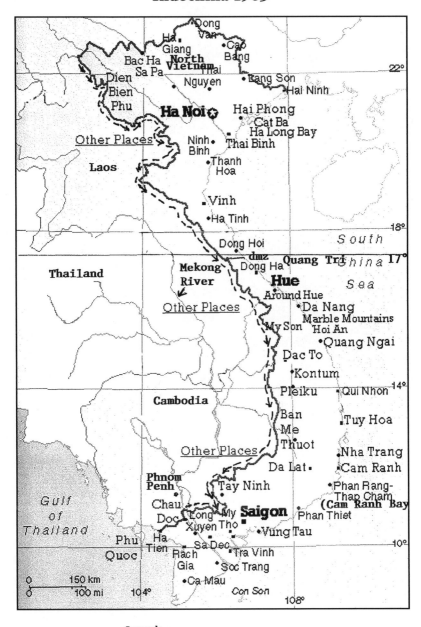

Legend:

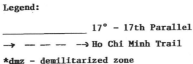

17° – 17th Parallel

→ — — — —→ Ho Chi Minh Trail

*dmz – demilitarized zone

Timeline

1945   Japan is expelled from Indochina and Ho Chi Minh sets up a provisional government.

1946   The Indochina War between the Vietnamese and the French begins. The U.S. supports France,

1954   The French suffer a devastating and ultimate defeat at Dien Bien Phu.

     By the Geneva <u>Accords</u>, North and South Vietnam are temporarily divided at the 17th parallel with the DMZ as a buffer zone.

     The <u>S.E.A.T.O.</u> pact is signed for the defense of Southeast Asia with the U.S. as the principal signatory.

1956   The French depart Indochina.

     The U.S. begins training South Vietnamese troops.

1959   First U.S. Military advisers enter Vietnam.

1960   The Communist National Liberation Front is officially formed in South Vietnam.

1961   President John F. Kennedy orders 3000 military advisers to South Vietnam.

Jan. 1962   American advisers join the Army of South Vietnam (ARVN) in their first combat against the Viet Cong.

1962   U.S. begins massive spraying of Agent Orange to clear thick vegetation shielding Viet Cong positions.

1963	With U.S. acquiescence, South Vietnamese President Ngo Dinh Diem is overthrown in a military coup and assassinated.
Early '64	The North Vietnamese Army (NVA) begins a massive drive to conquer South Vietnam, aided by Russia and China.
08/02/64	A North Vietnamese gunboat fires at a U.S. Naval Vessel patrolling the Gulf of Tonkin.
08/04/64	The Gulf of Tonkin Incident: USS Maddox reportedly fired upon by North Vietnam in the Gulf of Tonkin; U.S. launches retaliatory air strikes.
08/07/64	Congress passes the Gulf of Tonkin Resolution giving President Lyndon B. Johnson a blank check to conduct an undeclared war against the Viet Cong and North Vietnam.
11/01/64	Viet Cong shell Bien Hoa Airbase near Saigon.
01/01/65	A series of Viet Cong attacks throughout the south begins.
02/03/65	President Johnson launches Operation Rolling Thunder, bombing raids against North Vietnam to discourage its support of the Viet Cong.
1965	U.S. troops in Vietnam reach 200,000.
06/27/65	U.S. Commander in Vietnam, General William C. Westmoreland, launches first purely offensive operation by American ground forces.
08/17/65	Operation Starlight, the first major battle for the U.S., is an overwhelming victory.

11/14/65	<u>Battle of Ia Drang</u>, one of the largest battles of the war, results in 234 U.S. soldiers of the 1st Air Cavalry killed. Viet Cong casualties are in the thousands.
1966	U.S. and ARVN forces begin search and destroy missions against Viet Cong in the Mekong Delta.
05-06/66	<u>Battle of Dong Ha</u>
1966	6,000 U.S. Soldiers die in Vietnam in the year 1966.
1966	<u>Operation Cedar Falls</u> - Viet Cong driven out of the Iron Triangle near Saigon
1967	American bombing raids begin on North Vietnamese airfields at Hanoi and Haiphong.
01/21/68	The NVA attack and 77 day siege of the U.S. Marine Base at Khe San begins.
01/30/68	The NVA and Viet Cong commence the Tet offensive throughout South Vietnam; 37,000 Viet Cong troops are killed; 2,500 U.S. troops die in the offensive. It was simultaneously a military disaster for the Viet Cong and a public relations disaster for the United States.
02/1968	The Battle for Hué begins. The NVA executes 3,000 South Vietnamese civilians.
03/16/68	The My Lai Incident: 200 civilians are deliberately killed by U.S. troops, setting off a political firestorm.
04/1968	Citing opposition to the war, President Johnson announces he will not seek re-election.
06/1968	General Westmoreland approves the abandonment and demolition of the Khe Sanh Marine Base.

11/01/68	<u>Operation Rolling Thunder</u> ends.
02/1969	President Richard M. Nixon begins secret bombing of NVA and Viet Cong bases in Cambodia.
	Vietnamization policy announced by President Nixon to ease a transition to South Vietnamese takeover of war.
11/17/71	The Mansfield Amendment became law, requiring that the President set a date for the withdrawal of American forces from Indochina.
01/01/72	Only 133,000 U.S. servicemen remain in Vietnam. Most fighting is now conducted by the ARVN.
04/01/72	The NVA captures Northern Hué.
05/01/72	The NVA takes Quang Tri City.
1972	U.S. B-52s bomb Hanoi and Haiphong.
Late 1972	Only 24,200 U.S. troops are left in Vietnam.
01/27/73	Ceasefire signed in Paris.
03/1973	The last American combat troops leave Vietnam.
1974	The Viet Cong and NVA violate ceasefire repeatedly. With no American airpower to stop them, the NVA and VC make great gains.
04/30/75	Last Americans to die in Vietnam are two Marines killed at Tan Son Nhut Airport by NVA rocket fire.
04/30/75	The war ends after 15 years as Saigon falls to the NVA and Viet Cong. The last Americans evacuate the country.

Introduction

My tour of duty in Vietnam in 1966-67 as a United States Air Force officer was at the height of the American build-up in men, weapons, ships and planes.

Last Full Measure of Devotion captures that momentous time and place for me. I am particularly struck by how Farinacci adroitly weaves the stories of heroism with an overview of the history of the Vietnam War, while at the same time sidestepping most of the controversial aspects of public opinion and political debate of the day.

It is obvious that this was by design, in order to accentuate the fact that the depicted heroic actions were taken without hesitation or regard to the significant dissension over our role in Vietnam.

This is a book that finally recognizes and duly honors those individuals who served their country in the Vietnam War, with the highest sense of duty, patriotism, honor and bravery. War is hell and these stories vividly describe the horror and hell in their full dimensions.

I am simultaneously honored and humbled to provide this Introduction. How could I introduce a book about extraordinary heroism in combat when my unit in Vietnam acted in a non-combat support role, with the responsibility for maintenance and support of the C-130 Hercules aircraft? But, I realized that that is exactly the point. I had the distinction of being an eyewitness to history in the war zone where it all took place. This is a book about recognition and that recognition has to come from the vast majority of those who were not personally exposed to the level of combat experienced by those featured in this work.

The Hercules aircraft played a vital role. The air and ground crews had the huge and at times very dangerous task of transporting supplies and troops to our military operations throughout Vietnam. The Hercules notably played a major role in breaking the siege of the Marine base at Khe Sanh. The C-130 Hercules was large and relatively slow, providing an easy target for NVA planes and ground fire. We considered each and every mission to be critical and were acutely aware of the danger confronted by the crew each time the plane left the ground. This book is about a generation of heroes and many of the airmen I had the honor to serve with belong in their company.

I remain constantly proud of being a small but important part of our military's effort in Vietnam but especially proud of the bravery and patriotism of those individuals who in serving gave "their last full measure of devotion".

This tribute to America's heroes of the Vietnam War is not a treatise on the popularity or politics of that war. When called to serve in Vietnam our soldiers, marines, sailors and airmen did so because their country asked them and it was their unquestioned duty to do so. We were not attacked on our homeland but we were honoring an agreement, SEATO, to protect those countries against the spread of communism, an ideology in opposition to our principles of democracy. As a result we committed our country's military to the Vietnam conflict to prevent the "Domino Theory" from becoming reality, to halt the spread of communism in South East Asia.

All wars, popular or not, have their share of heroes. But for whatever reason because of the stigma that surrounds this war there hasn't been the appropriate recognition of these heroic efforts. This is probably because of the perception, right or wrong, that the war was unjust or just bungled. Even today, some 40 plus years later, it is often referred to as an example of what we don't want to do. But to those who served with devotion we owe the highest level of respect and gratitude that can be bestowed upon them. There was no hesitation on their part in discharging their duties regardless of the public or political opinion.

May we as individuals and as a country never fail to remember all those who serve in our military, giving recognition to all their sacrifices, and especially to those who gave their "last full measure of devotion" so that all of us can enjoy the benefits of a democracy.

William F. Christ

CHAPTER I
Heroes or Headliners?

There are few words in the English language which have become more elastic in their meaning than "hero". The word is liberally applied to a great variety of activities, many of which are primarily self-serving. The quarterback who throws the winning touchdown or the centerfielder who strokes the game-winning homerun is called the "hero" of the game. Conversely, the running back who commits the game-costing fumble or the shortstop whose errant throw causes his team to lose the World Series, has pinned on him the label which is the modern day opposite of a hero - the "goat". But, suppose the "goat" gave up his body for the good of the team by diving into the dirt to field the ball before making his errant throw? No matter - he's still the goat because he lost. And, what if the quarterback had an incentive-laden contract which paid him an extra twenty thousand dollars for each touchdown pass and as a result he passed up a safer, less spectacular play? That inconvenient detail would likely not even be reported by the sports media. Who cares? He's the "hero", because he won. Something is askew in our cultural values.

For every truly heroic cop or firefighter who puts his life on the line to save or protect others, there is the ersatz hero whose floor to ceiling poster might adorn a teenager's bedroom wall or door - that of the action movie star or mega-rock star. Posters of hero soldiers, police officers or firefighters are not likely to grace too many bedroom walls or doors.

This book extols the generosity and bravery of real heroes, not phony ones - not war movie heroes who themselves skillfully dodged the draft.

Like the ideal hero of Greek mythology and legend, the men depicted in the pages that follow did extremely dangerous things to help others. Though some of their actions, like falling on hand grenades or charging head-on into enemy small arms fire, seem almost suicidal, they did not seek to die and they did not want to die. As they saw it, it wasn't about them. For some of them it was about saving or protecting a buddy, a squad, a platoon or a company. For others, it was about saving or protecting innocent non-combatants.

For still others, it was about how they saw their duty to their country. But, whatever their motivation, it did not stem from vainglorious and reckless bravado. These military heroes were more akin to the firefighters who climbed up the stairs of the World Trade Center's blazing and crumbling twin towers on September 11, 2001, while almost everyone else was climbing down the stairs to safety. Those valiant firefighters had no less desire to survive and live than the civilians rushing to safety. It was just that they had chosen an occupation that called for great love and generosity, even to the point of sacrificing their own lives so others could survive. Like the firefighters of 9/11, like the construction worker who threw himself on the New York subway tracks to protect a stranger who had fallen during a seizure, the heroes of this book gave and gave until they had exhausted their last full measure of devotion.

CHAPTER II
Genesis 1945-1960

The seeds of America's involvement in the Vietnam conflict were planted and nurtured in the Cold War between the United States and its allies on one side and the Soviet Union and Communist China on the other, a conflict which began shortly after the end of World War II and lasted more than forty years.

Although Winston Churchill is accurately credited with having coined the phrase "Iron Curtain", George Kennan, United States Ambassador to Russia, was the first to articulate a United States policy to check further communist expansion.

In the summer of 1947, Kennan's article published in the *Journal of Foreign Affairs* introduced the idea of "containment". He recommended "a policy of firm containment [of Russia] with unalterable counterforce at every point where the Russians show signs of encroaching..." Although Kennan ultimately opposed applying containment on the Asian mainland, the idea of containment provided the philosophical and strategic underpinnings of the Truman Doctrine, the Marshall Plan, the Berlin Airlift, U.S. opposition to the Communist revolution in China and America's involvement in the Korean and Vietnam Wars.

Faced with the movement by the Soviet Union in the aftermath of World War II to overturn Eastern European governments and replace them with Communist regimes, President Truman enunciated what would become the cornerstone of American policy during the Cold War:

"It must be the policy of the United States to support free peoples who are resisting attempted subjugation by armed minorities or by outside pressures."

This statement, known as The Truman Doctrine, became embedded in the foreign policies of Presidents Harry S. Truman, Dwight D. Eisenhower, John F. Kennedy, Lyndon B. Johnson, and Richard M. Nixon. The contemporaneous occurrences of Soviet hegemony over most of Eastern Europe and victory by the communist forces of Mao Tse-Tung on the mainland of China in the late 1940's, fortified the widely held perception in the West of a monolithic international communist threat to dominate the world. To disregard this context when assessing both the Korean and Vietnam Wars is to ignore history. The prevention of further inroads by the Soviets and Communist Chinese was the bedrock of U.S. foreign policy in the late 40's, 50's, and 60's. There is little doubt that the American people were at least initially willing to expend their blood and treasure to this end. Consider John F. Kennedy's universally acclaimed Inaugural Address in which he pledged "to pay any price, to bear any burden, to meet any hardship, in the defense of freedom."

Red China's and Soviet Russia's support of the communist government in North Korea and the communist movement in Indochina in the early 1950's only served to lend credence to the perception of a threat of World-wide communist domination. After the unsuccessful French effort in fighting the communist Viet Minh in Indochina, climaxed by the fall of Dien Bien Phu in 1954, U.S. Secretary of State, John Foster Dulles, conceived the Southeast Asia Treaty Organization (S.E.A.T.O.), composed of the United States, Great Britain, France, Australia, Thailand and Pakistan, to defend Southeast Asia. The French who believed they would retain some influence in the South were totally supplanted by the U.S. in the aftermath of S.E.A.T.O. A protocol to the treaty put South Vietnam, (formerly part of Indochina), Cambodia and Laos under its protection. A regional security arrangement was devised and then formalized in the "Geneva Accords." Nevertheless, the Viet Cong, the successor to the Viet Minh, was loosely in place in South Vietnam by 1954. Throughout the remainder of the 1950's, and into the early 60's, the United States provided substantial support to prop up the non-communist Ngo Dinh Diem regime in South Vietnam, while China and the Soviet Union supported the leftist regime of Ho Chi Minh in North Vietnam, and its sponsored insurgency in South Vietnam. From 1954 on, the regime in South Vietnam was in a continuous state of guerrilla war with the Viet Cong and North Vietnam.

In the early 1960's, China and Russia dramatically increased their military aid to North Vietnam, thereby strengthening the insurrection against the Diem regime in the South. The United States led by Presidents John F. Kennedy and Lyndon Baines Johnson, Secretary of State Dean Rusk, and Secretary of Defense Robert R. McNamara, in turn increased its assistance, first by sending a large number of military advisers to assist the Army of the Republic of Vietnam (ARVN) and, ultimately, after the Gulf of Tonkin incident on August 4, 1964, by placing ground troops in South Vietnam. President Johnson eventually sent 540,000 U.S. soldiers to Vietnam. The greatest expansion of our military presence there occurred in 1965 and 1966 after the North Vietnamese Army began major attacks, with the objective of totally conquering South Vietnam.

The United States' effort in Vietnam was an attempt to contain communist expansion and thereby prevent the fall of yet another domino in a string of Cold War losses dating back to the years immediately following World War II, while at the same time honoring a treaty obligation. But, first and foremost, containment was the framework for the Korean and Vietnam Wars. Whether the effort was necessary and justified is a topic for some other book and on this question, much has been written, both pro and con. Nevertheless, fidelity to history compels the observation that unlike the colonialism of the French, the conquest of the Japanese and the aggressive communism of the Soviet Union, the U.S. role in Southeast Asia emanated from a defensive, not offensive, foreign policy (i.e. containment). Notably, the same guerrillas who ultimately were our enemies from 1961 to 1975 were our allies against the Japanese during World War II.

Although America lost in Vietnam, it ultimately won the Cold War. How much our effort in Vietnam contributed to the ultimate victory is for historians and non-historians alike to ponder. Whatever the answer, it in no way diminishes the valiant effort made by our fighting forces in that forlorn corner of the world; and the duty they performed for their country should not be devalued by anyone's negative view of America's role.

The foundation of a nation will surely crumble without legions of young men and women willing to put their lives on the line when their country calls. Hence, irrespective of the merit or lack of merit of the cause in which they were called, those who answered that call did well for their country simply because they did their duty.

"All those who enter the military in service of their country should look upon themselves as guardians of the security and freedom of their fellow countrymen, and in carrying out this duty properly, they, too, contribute to the establishment of peace."

Second Vatican Council of The Roman Catholic Church

CHAPTER III
The Early Years 1961 - 1964

Southeast Asia, since the end of World War II, had been in ferment. The nascent communist movement dating back to well before World War II had been temporarily on hold while all interests, including Chinese, British, French, American and Indochinese united to defeat the Japanese invaders.

After the final defeat of Japan by the allies in 1945, however, leftist leaders such Ho Chi Minh and Vo Nguyen Giap resumed their campaign to supplant French colonial rule in Indochina with communist domination. The United States was able to hold Ho Chi Minh and his legions at bay through the 1950's by imposing through the S.E.A.T.O. Pact, a temporary division of Vietnam into two regimes -North and South. By 1961, however, indigenous political/military movements such as the Pathet Lao in Laos, the Khmer Rouge in Cambodia and the Viet Minh (later Viet Cong) in South Vietnam were mounting serious insurrections against the shaky regimes of Southeast Asia.

American President John F. Kennedy who had campaigned as an internationalist had suffered a humiliating defeat in early 1961 against the Soviet-backed regime in Cuba, at the Bay of Pigs. Unwilling to suffer another defeat in Laos as the Pathet Lao in 1961 threatened the pro-Western regime in Laos, President Kennedy decided against U.S. military intervention there. A coalition government was subsequently formed.

Kennedy could not, however, ignore the deterioration of conditions in South Vietnam, nor did he want to. An astute student of international politics, he was fully aware of Resolution 15 of the Central Committee of the Vietnamese Communist Party, which stated: "The way to carry out the Vietnamese revolution in the South is through the use of violence."[1]

To realize this objective, Ho Chi Minh engineered the formation of the National Liberation Front of South Vietnam on December 20, 1960, to foment a leftist revolution of the people against the Diem regime.

In 1961 there began a mass infiltration from North Vietnam via the Ho Chi Minh Trail into the South, of revitalized Viet Minh units, which had been lying dormant in the North since the armistice with the French in 1954.

Soon they were occupying and controlling regions in the South along the border with Cambodia, in the Central Highlands and in the Mekong Delta. If nothing was done to curb their progress, cities such as Hué, Quang Tri, Dakto, Pleiku and eventually Saigon would be in great jeopardy. Now styled the Viet Cong, these well-armed and well-trained militia used violence and assassination against civilian leaders and those among the general populace who would not support them.

The anticommunist Diem regime and its corrupt and ineffective Army of the Republic of Vietnam (ARVN) were in deep trouble and appealed urgently to the United States for help. President Kennedy, frustrated by U.S. inability to thwart the leftist movement in Laos, seized the opportunity to take dramatic action by sending three thousand U.S. military advisers to South Vietnam in 1961, to help mold the ARVN into an effective fighting force. After Kennedy's assassination in Dallas on November 22, 1963, President Johnson continued the slow but steady build-up of American advisers in South Vietnam.

At the same time, Ho Chi Minn was stepping up activity in the South. The first full Viet Cong infantry regiment was formed on November 20, 1962, ultimately composed of four battalions. Named the 1st Infantry Regiment and comprised mainly of professional soldiers, the regiment spent most of 1963 in training and engaged in a few small battles with the ARVN. In 1964, however, perhaps because of a greater sense of urgency caused by more and more U.S. advisers in place in the South, particularly after the Gulf of Tonkin Resolution, the 1st Regiment fought three major battles against the ARVN, emerging victorious in all of them.

In 1963 the corrupt Diem regime of South Vietnam fell in a military coup, secretly unopposed by the U.S.; and President Diem was assassinated. Political stability, however, did not follow. A parade of undistinguished leaders ascended to the position of President, some serving only a couple of months, as the U.S. tried to bring about the installation of a credible regime in South Vietnam. The lack of political stability in the South only encouraged the Viet Cong and North Vietnam to step up their political and military offensives in 1964 and in the first half of 1965.

In the summer of 1964, an important decision was being made in Hanoi. The more aggressive leaders in the defense establishment pushed hard for the introduction into the South of several divisions of the North Vietnamese People's Army. Their goal was to conquer and rule the southern part of what they always saw as one country, Vietnam; and not two separate countries divided at the 17th parallel. To accomplish this mission, they believed that providing arms and supplies to a guerrilla movement was simply not enough. They yearned to seize the opportunity to meet the weaker ARVN units on the battlefield with strong NVA forces who would smash them and little by little "liberate" key parts of the South.

General Vo Nguyen Giap opposed the plan of escalation as ill-conceived and premature and urged a continuation of the guerrilla-war phase, which had proved successful. President Ho Chi Minh, however, backed the plan of escalation and ordered its full implementation, to take place in 1965.

The posture of the U.S. military in Vietnam did not go from a passive advisory role to an active combat role overnight. Instead, a gradual transition took place. As early as January 12, 1962, American advisers joined the ARVN in their first all-out combat against the Viet Cong. As early as 1961, U.S. Special Forces advisers were leading Montagnard tribesmen in the mountains of the Central Highlands in battles against the VC*.

* short for Viet Cong

This was a no-brainer for U.S. military strategists since the Montagnards, skilled mercenary soldiers, hated ethnic Vietnamese of all stripes, whether VC, Northern or Southern. As soldiers, the Montagnards were brave and highly effective in their home territory and teamed with the Green Berets made for a formidable fighting force.

But, 1965 was the year the U.S. truly began full-scale combat operations with U.S. forces as the major participants, beginning shortly after a series of Viet Cong attacks throughout January of 1965.

In a reverse historical parallel, unlike the timid and ineffective forays of Union General George B. McClellan, against Lee's Army of Northern Virginia in 1861, the U.S. fought the VC and the NVA in earnest in 1965. They, in fact, either initiated or participated in major battles, such as the Marine victory in Operation Starlight in August of 1965 and the 7th Air Cavalry engagement in the Battle of Ia Drang Valley in November of that year. Both those encounters are treated elsewhere in this book.

In sum, the early years, 1961 through 1964, comprised a period of equivocation and tentative resolve by the U.S., gradually hardening into a determination by the Johnson Administration to deny Ho Chi Minn his fervently desired victory.

Humberto Roque Versace

"...We must be imprisoned but must we whine as well? ...My leg you will chain-yes, but my will -no, not even Zeus can conquer that....You do what you have to do and I'll do what I have to do, which is to live and die like a man."

Epictetus, Roman stoic philosopher

There is no way of knowing if Humberto Roque Versace ever heard of the great Roman philosopher, Epictetus, but I feel certain that if he had known and read Epictetus he would have found him to be a kindred spirit. After all, they shared the common experience of having as young men been imprisoned and tortured by brutal and unjust captors. Faced with this ordeal, both of them looked their tormentors in the eye and defied them to try to take away even the smallest measure of their humanity. Like Epictetus, Humberto Roque Versace knew himself, and knew at what level he placed his worth. Perhaps even more than Epictetus, he knew the rightness of his cause and dedicated himself to it with unflagging courage and self-sacrifice.

Humberto Versace, nicknamed "Rocky", was steeped in the U.S. Army tradition of duty, honor and country. As a graduate of the United States Military Academy at West Point, one would expect him to be imbued with the concept of honor and duty above self. As a devout Christian, one might also attribute the extraordinary strength and courage demonstrated by Versace in Vietnam to his powerful faith. But, to find the formula for what made Rocky Versace tick in his military credo and Christian beliefs would be far too *easy*. There is never any facile explanation for what makes men like Rocky Versace the way they are. Where do such men come from? Perhaps it is only in the peculiar facts of their stories themselves that we have any chance of finding a clue to their inner workings.

Versace was one of the group of early United States military advisers designated to teach, advise and work with the South Vietnamese government in combating the communist insurgents. As a member of the United States Army Special Forces, he volunteered for service in Vietnam in 1962 before there were any U.S. combat troops there, and at a time when there were only a few thousand such military advisers in all of South Vietnam.

As an intelligence adviser in the Mekong Delta, Versace quickly became immersed in Vietnamese culture. It was obvious that he saw his role as encompassing far more than just military advice and training. He threw himself into the types of tasks which later were incorporated into the "pacification" program of the Pentagon and General William Westmoreland, Commanding General of U.S. forces in Vietnam. Versace established dispensaries, worked hard to improve village playgrounds and procured tin sheeting to replace thatched roofs. He even convinced schools in the United States to contribute soccer balls for the village children.

After almost completing his first one-year tour in Vietnam, Versace volunteered for a second tour. His long-range plans called for him to leave the army upon completion of his second one year tour and enter the priesthood. He had already been accepted into the Maryknoll Order of the Roman Catholic Church. He hoped to be able to return to Vietnam as a priest and continue his work with Vietnamese children.

Humberto Versace never fulfilled his dream, but instead became one of the approximately 200 prisoners, mostly infantry soldiers, held in captivity by the communist insurgents in jungle camps in South Vietnam, where they were forced to endure the most atrocious conditions imaginable.

In the army, a "short timer" is often seen as a person to be envied because he is approaching the end of his tour of duty. Rocky Versace was as short a timer as you can be in October of 1963. With only two weeks to go in his tour in Vietnam, he accompanied a unit of the South Vietnamese Army on patrol. During the operation, they encountered a large enemy force. A firefight ensued, and Versace went down with three rounds in the leg. He and two other Americans were taken prisoners. Despite being wounded, he and the others were stripped of their boots and led off on a march through the jungle to a Viet Cong confinement area.

The prisoners' cells were bamboo cages. The men were consistently malnourished, subjected to appallingly unsanitary conditions, exposed to heat, insects and disease, and deprived of medical attention. Versace's untreated leg became badly infected. This did not stop him, however, from attempting to escape. Within three weeks after his capture, he crawled away *on* his hands and knees. He was recaptured and as part of his punishment, the guards twisted his injured leg.

After his escape attempt, Versace was placed in irons, and forced to lay flat on his back, in a dark and hot bamboo isolation cage, 6 feet by 2 feet and 3 feet high. In his confinement, he was frequently gagged.

A lesser man might have had his will broken by such treatment and become totally submissive to his captor's demands. This was not the case with Rocky Versace, a man made of sterner stuff. He attended Viet Cong indoctrination classes only at the tip of a bayonet. The prisoners were uniformly besieged by wrenching bouts of dysentery and, in the midst of their suffering, some of them adopted a sit-and-listen attitude in the classes. Versace, to the contrary, hurled verbal challenges at his would-be Communist indoctrinators. Possessed of finely honed skills in persuasive speaking, he would take on all comers and tie his so-called instructors up in linguistic knots by the sheer strength of his talent for argumentation and debate. Over and over Versace would trip up the Viet Cong instructors with his verbal gymnastics. His defiance of his captivity, however, was not simply verbal.

Versace made three more escape attempts and with each attempt his treatment worsened and became more brutal.

The last time his fellow prisoners heard his voice, Rocky Versace was singing "God Bless America" at the top of his lungs from his isolation box. By then he had become a real threat to the NVA and VC prisoner indoctrination programs - he was a thorn in their sides and they wanted to be rid of him.

On September 28, 1969, Hanoi Radio announced that Humberto Roque Versace, a man who his tormentors could not break or even bend, had been executed. Had he lived and died in the times of the great and stalwart stoic philosophers, such as Epictetus, Xeno and Marcus Aurelius, he would undoubtedly have been viewed as a role model. Do great men and women create the events of their times, or is it the historical events which create their greatness? Whatever the answer, Humberto Roque Versace's story is an epic tale of a short life, well lived; in fact, lived with greatness.

Humberto Roque Versace, a little-known American hero, was ultimately awarded posthumously the highest honor his country can confer, the Medal of Honor.

South Vietnam, Early 1964

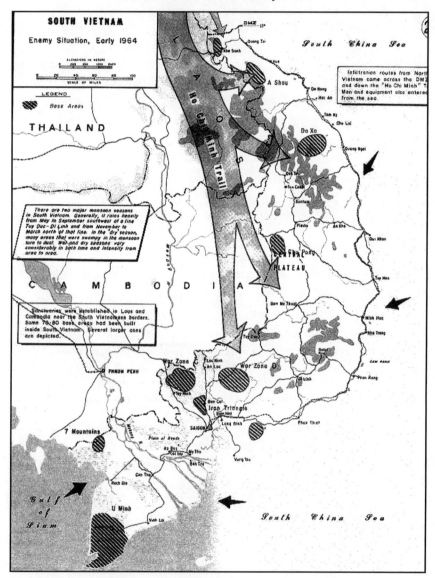

CHAPTER IV
America at War, 1965

The entire U.S. posture in Southeast Asia underwent a metamorphosis in 1965. In the face of a series of Viet Cong attacks in the South beginning in early January, President Johnson and General Westmoreland, armed with their new authority under the Tonkin Resolution, were anxious to flex some real U.S. muscle.

Hence, in February of 1965, Johnson launched Operation Rolling Thunder, a campaign of bombing raids against North Vietnam designed to discourage its support of the Viet Cong offensive in the South.

U.S. troops "in country" approached the 200,000 mark as General Westmoreland simultaneously launched the first purely offensive operation by American ground forces.

The U.S. offensive came none too soon since by the end of 1964 General Giap had three full Viet Cong divisions within fifty miles of Saigon, meeting with little resistance from the ARVN. By February of 1965 the Viet Cong had taken control over vast segments of the highways, railroads and other key infrastructure of South Vietnam. The U.S. backed Thieu regime was close to a total collapse and takeover by the National Liberation Front (NLF) and its sponsor to the north.

Against this backdrop, the United States Marines hit the shore, landing on the coast of the South China Sea, south of Danang, with a mission to protect the U.S. airfield at Chu Lai. Under the command of Lieutenant Colonel Joseph R. "Bull" Fisher, the 2nd Battalion, 4th

Marines, came ashore on the morning of May 7, 1965. They moved swiftly onto the beach from their landing crafts with weapons locked and loaded. Encountering no resistance, the battalion quickly moved inland, secured National Route 1 along the coast and established a command post near the northwest corner of the Chu Lai airfield. Outposts were immediately established and patrols sent out with dispatch.

By June of 1965, military intelligence had detected the presence of elements of two North Vietnamese Army (NVA) divisions operating in the South. In response to his urgent requests to Washington for help, General Westmoreland was advised by the Pentagon that fifty-four additional combat battalions would be sent from continental United States as soon as possible. At about the same time, President Johnson and the Pentagon decided to use the Marines in combat for the first time.

Events were moving at a breakneck pace and the atmosphere was ripe for a major squaring-off between U.S. forces and the NVA/Viet Cong. It would soon come.

1. Operation Starlight - By Land and By Sea

The 1965 U.S. Marine combined sea, ground and air assault on the Viet Cong, reminiscent of the World War II battles on Guadalcanal, Iwo Jima and Okinawa, had its origins in a fortuitous and isolated event. On August 15, 1965 a single VC soldier captured by the ARVN revealed the dramatic news that the 1st Viet Cong Regiment, notorious for its ruthlessness, was preparing for a major assault upon the Marine base at Chu Lai, with its strategically valuable airfield. According to the VC informant, it was to be a two-pronged attack - the main force would attack and attempt to destroy the airfield buildings, structures and aircraft while a sizeable force of VC guerrillas would engage the defenders in a firefight, with the hope of pinning them down and locking them in place while the main assault was carried out.[i]

The top Marine in Vietnam, the highly respected General Louis Walt, upon being advised by intelligence that the informant's reliability was high and the information itself was corroborated by other sources, had a tough decision to make. He could either meticulously plan and prepare for a defense of the Chu Lai base or plan and execute a preemptive attack against the Viet Cong. General Walt, knowing that it was only a matter of time before he would have to fight the VC head-on decided to do so on his own terms by taking the fight to the enemy. The method chosen was a combined amphibious and helicopter operation. The name chosen was "Operation Starlight". D day was scheduled for 18 August and H hour would be 0630 hours.[ii] The landing force would embark from three ships in the South China Sea off the coast of Quang Ngai. The ships would provide supporting naval gunfire to the landing troops.

The Battle

The three ships dropped anchor shortly after 0500 hours and the assault boats hit the beaches on schedule. The VC had not anticipated an amphibious landing and were forced to scramble to put troops in position to fight a blocking action, designed to keep the Marines from overrunning the VC command post, until the VC had time to vacate to a new position further inland.

The VC also failed to foresee how quickly the Marines would move forward on all fronts. Thus, as the VC moved to defend against the amphibious assault by 3rd Battalion, 3rd Marines (3/3), Captain Mike Morris's "Mike Company" had already moved into position inland along a ridgeline to the north of the main Viet Cong position, from where Mike Company would act as a blocking force. The plan was brilliant in its simplicity. The amphibious landing force and Bull Fisher's 2/4, the helicopter landing force to the south of the main objective, were the hammers which would drive the VC towards Mike Company, the anvil. The VC regiment would thereby be trapped by a three-pronged pincer movement.

Mike Company had reached its objective without incident at around 0230 hours on August 18th and immediately dug in. Its blocking position, which included a battery of six 107 mm. howitzers, was ready for action by 0630 hours.

The 2/4 Commander, Joseph R. "Bull" Fisher, was a legendary Marine hero of Iwo Jima during World War II where he won the Silver Star, and at Chosen Reservoir in Korea where he was awarded the Navy Cross. He was an aging but tough and tireless leader whose men respected him fully, and proudly called themselves "The Magnificent Bastards". Fisher selected three main landing zones. Echo Company of the 2/4 was put down at LZ "White" in the center of his three companies in the field. Golf Company landed to the North (LZ "Red") and Hotel Company to the South (LZ "Blue").

Robert E. O'Malley

Meanwhile, the assault boats and amphibious tractors of the 3/3 approached the beach. In their Amtrak, the members of Corporal Robert E. O'Malley's squad waited in tightly-coiled tension with weapons locked and loaded. They had no idea what awaited them on the beach, but as soon as the ramp was dropped, the combination of superb training, excellent conditioning and nervous energy propelled them out of the craft, onto the beach and into a rapid forward advance.

Miles inland, Bull Fisher's air-assault battalion was running into heavy VC small-arms and mortar assaults as they moved in a northeasterly direction from their landing zones. Second Platoon of Hotel Company attacked the VC defensive position on Hill 43 but under heavy VC fire made it only to the bottom of the hill.

Third platoon did no better on its first foray against the VC occupied village, Nam Yen 3. VC grenades exploded and arms fire cut into the advancing Third Platoon, which was forced to fall back. But, while Hotel Company's embattled warriors were bogged down, Easy Company was advancing without impediment, which ironically threatened to undo any semblance of a coordinated overall advance, by moving too far out in front of Hotel and Golf Companies. This didn't lessen Easy Company's effectiveness, however, as they were able to call in massive artillery strikes upon a heavy concentration of VC up ahead of Easy, resulting in heavy enemy casualties, including many VC killed.

The amphibious arm of the three-pronged pincer operation, spearheaded by India Company, 3rd Battalion, 3rd Marines, was moving quickly inland in the direction of the village of An Cuong 2. A group of M48 tanks had landed in the second wave. Corporal O'Malley's squad was assigned to the tanks and eagerly climbed on board. Perhaps seeking to outflank the Viet Cong concentration at An Cuong 2, the tank commander directed his section away from the main body of India Company and along a trench line to the West of the main Marine assault. O'Malley's squad of nine or ten men was divided roughly evenly among the three tanks, with O'Malley, Lance Corporal Chris Buchs, and PFC Robert Rimpson on the lead tank. O'Malley and his men were sitting ducks astride the tanks, but as they moved around a large hedgerow with no VC opposition apparent, they could tell from the noise of small arms fire and grenades to the northeast that the main Marine amphibious attack force was in a major battle, of the sort O'Malley's squad had thus far avoided. The hedgerow seemed to be affording the tanks some concealment and for the first time since they boarded the landing craft, the men of Corporal O'Malley's squad actually felt a sense of optimism and confidence that their mission would be successfully accomplished without major casualties. This positive mood ended rudely and abruptly when without warning three BAR rounds tore into Lance Corporal Merlin Marquart, who was sitting on top of the middle tank, mortally wounding the young Marine. Despite frantic efforts by Corporal O'Malley and other squad members to administer life-saving first aid and to find a medic, Corporal Marquart died of his wounds on the ground near the middle tank.

As they worked on Marquart the squad also poured suppressing fire and tossed grenades into the hedgerow. The VC were well-entrenched on the other side of the hedgerow, however, and the hand grenades either bounced off the hedge or exploded harmlessly within the thick bamboo and foliage.

Suddenly, the alert Buchs spotted a narrow opening in the hedgerow. "I'll cover you while you move through shouted Buchs to O'Malley." "Well let's go Buchs" was O'Malley's reply.[iii] Neither Buchs nor O'Malley had any idea what they would be up against on the other side of the hedgerow; yet without hesitation O'Malley dashed through the opening with Buchs right on his heels. On the other side they jumped into a long trench. Buchs took the left side of the trench, O'Malley the right and together they poured a barrage of rifle fire and grenades at the surprised and overwhelmed VC. Within brief minutes twelve VC lay dead in the trench, eight of them shot by O'Mally and four by Buchs. By then Corporal Haydn and Private First-Class Rimpson had joined Buchs and O'Malley, and as O'Malley moved forward along the left side of the trench with Haydn behind him, a VC who had been feigning death by lying still at the bottom of the trench suddenly jumped up and threw a grenade at Haydn. The explosion wounded both O'Malley and Hayden - Haydn took a fragment in the hip and O'Malley took one in the foot. Rimpson killed the remaining VC with his grenade launcher and the battle of the trench was over. O'Malley, though wounded, refused to be evacuated and elected to stay with his men .

Simultaneously, the main amphibious force of 3/3 was successfully assaulting and capturing An Cuong 2. More than 40 VC died in the battle.

O'Malley rallied his squad and even though the tanks were under assault from anti-armor fire, they managed to get the wounded squad members back on the tanks and continued their forward advance. But, before long, they started receiving heavy small-arms fire and some of the wounded were hit for a second time. O'Malley knew the Marines had an advantage if they could only exploit their superior tank fire-power. He then saw an opportunity and acted on it by leaping into the bushes from where he had a better line of vision. He proceeded to point out VC targets to the tank crews. Suddenly, several mortar rounds landed among the tanks and the vehicles began to back up. By then, O'Malley and his men were in the trench and he knew what was coming next. As the tanks fell back the VC fired mortars into the trench. O'Malley and Buchs tried to get out but were blown back into the trench by mortar rounds landing a few yards away, and O'Malley took a second hit in his forearm. Instead of giving himself the last best chance of surviving by getting himself out of the trench immediately, O'Malley ignored his wounds and proceeded to drag another wounded Marine out of the trench, while ordering Buchs and Rimpson to do the same for a second man.

At a separate venue, the other part of the hammer was hitting the VC hard. Hotel Company, 2/4 had secured Hill. 43 and was on the move toward Nam Yen 3. The VC were taking heavy losses everywhere.

Corporal O'Malley and the survivors of his squad were attempting to rejoin India Company, 3/3. They came under attack again and as O'Malley led his men to a defensive position in a rice paddy, he took another round, this time in the chest. They didn't stay in a defensive posture for long because Medevac Helicopters were being prevented from landing by a .30 caliber VC machine gun on a hill. O'Malley and his men moved against the machine gun, pouring heavy fire into the VC position as the Medevac bird landed. Rimpson was wounded in the eye and his resulting poor vision prevented him from knocking out the machine gun. O'Malley kept firing at the hill, but probably because of his three wounds, was also unable to knock it out. Finally, Buchs took Rimpson's weapon and took out the machine gun on his second shot.

O'Malley again refused evacuation as the first Medevac helicopter went out with seven Marines on board. O'Malley and the rest of India

Company kept intense fire on the VC—held hill as the aircraft took off. O'Malley finally went out on the second Medevac flight. It was on that flight that Buchs discovered for the first time that he too had been wounded in the chest. The actions taken by O'Malley, Buchs, Rimpson, and other members of their squad during Operation Starlight had been extraordinary. Sixteen months later, President Johnson presented Robert E. O'Malley with the Medal of Honor. He was the first Marine recipient of that award of the Vietnam War.

Joe C. Paul

The toughest resistance from the Viet Cong in Operation Starlight was experienced by Hotel Company 2/4 of the air-assault prong of the operation. After several attempts, however, they finally overran and secured Hill 43, and were then able to turn their full attention to Nam Yen 3. But, before they could do that, Second Platoon was pinned down by automatic and small-arms fire plus a fierce mortar barrage. As First Platoon advanced on the VC position, Lance Corporal Joe C. Paul, though himself wounded, was left behind to protect other wounded Marines. But, the VC had other ideas as they determinedly poured fire into the group of wounded men lying on the ground. It had appeared only minutes before that young Lance Corporal Joe Calvin Paul would not be in a position to help his wounded comrades. But, the kid from Kentucky possessed the quiet demeanor, yet steely resolve and fearlessness of so many of his coon-skin capped ancestors who had tamed and settled the Kentucky wilderness. Paul had actually been on a Medevac chopper but courageously took himself off when he saw that help was needed.

The situation of the wounded and their guardian angel, Lance Corporal Paul, was getting desperate. The VC were throwing everything at them - recoilless rifle fire, mortars, small arms fire and most frightening of all, white phosphorous grenades launched from special rifles. Contact by the phosphorous with human skin produces burns which eat through the dermal layers, even underwater.[iv]

Paul knew that if he didn't act immediately they would all die painful deaths where they lay. Suddenly, as if shot from a cannon, he dashed across a rice paddy directly into the teeth of the enemy fire, positioning himself between the VC and the wounded Marines, all the while smothering the VC position with automatic rifle fire. He desperately needed to buy his buddies enough time for them to be safely evacuated, and hopefully lay down enough suppressing fire to save himself as well. He was a man possessed, on a perilous mission and in grave danger, yet unrelenting in his zeal. He was fearless himself and fearsome to his enemy. Paul was a throwback to the mountain men of early 18th century Kentucky, almost as if he were armed with a single shot musket against scores of attacking Creek Indians, busy filling the air with a deadly rain of arrows.

After taking hits from enemy fire three or four times, Paul must have known that any fleeting hopes he had of getting out alive were now gone. But, he and his weapon had become one, a relentless fighting machine, inexorably moving forward, programmed to advance only, in permanent attack mode. Only after all the wounded were pulled on to the Medevac chopper did he go down, felled by his many wounds. A brave fellow Marine, Corporal Dick Tonucci, was able to pick Paul up and get him onto a Medevac chopper.[v] But, Corporal Paul didn't make it. True, he was an extraordinary hero who had sacrificed himself to save the wounded soldiers under his charge. But, he also had become a lonely statistic - one of 58,000 slain Americans of the Vietnam War .

Lance Corporal Joe Calvin Paul did not remain an anonymous statistic for long. He was posthumously awarded the Medal of Honor by President Johnson, and the naval ship, the USS Paul, was named in his honor.

At the end of the day, Operation Starlight was a huge victory for U.S. forces. Ironically, it was also a watershed for the Viet Cong. After Operation Starlight the VC seldom, if ever, took on U.S. forces in direct, open combat. They learned that they could not compete against the sophisticated weaponry and superior fire power of the Americans. They also learned that guerrilla warfare on their own terrain was a far more effective tactic, a means of neutralizing the U.S. and ARVN advantage in weaponry.

In this sense, Operation Starlight was at once the first major battle by the United States in Vietnam and a turning point for the highly adaptable Viet Cong in their strategy and tactics.

The Battle of Ia Drang

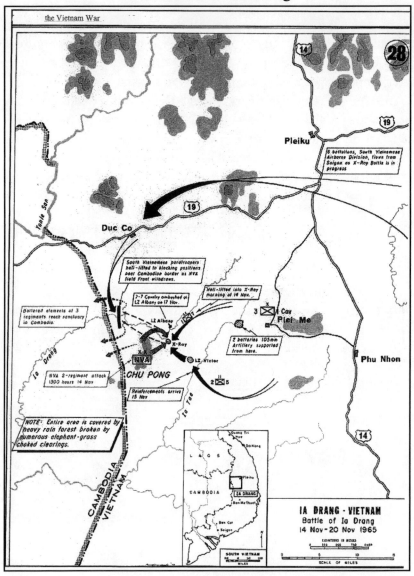

28

14

19

Pleiku

6 battalions, South Vietnamese Airborne Division, flown from Saigon as X-Ray Battle is in progress

19

Duc Co

South Vietnamese paratroopers heli-lifted to blocking positions near Cambodian border as NVA field Front withdraws.

Tanle San

2-7 Cavalry ambushed at LZ Albany on 17 Nov.

Heli-lifted into X-Ray morning of 14 Nov.

Battered elements of 3 regiments reach sanctuary in Cambodia.

3 Cav
Plei Me

LZ Albany

X-Ray

2 batteries 105mm Artillery supported from here.

Ia Drang

NVA

Phu Nhon

LZ Victor

NVA 3-regiment attack 1300 hours 14 Nov

CHU PONG

2 5

Reinforcements arrive 15 Nov.

Ia Tae

NOTE: Entire area is covered by heavy rain forest broken by numerous elephant-grass choked clearings.

14

CAMBODIA
VIETNAM

Quang Tri
Hue
Da Nang

L A O S

Pleiku

CAMBODIA

IA DRANG

Ban Me Thuot

Ban Cot

Saigon

SOUTH VIETNAM

MILES

IA DRANG - VIETNAM
Battle of Ia Drang
14 Nov - 20 Nov 1965

ELEVATIONS IN METERS

SCALE OF MILES

2. The Battle of Ia Drang - Into the Valley of Death

Storm'd with shot and shell Boldly they rode and well Into the jaws of Death Into the mouths of Hell.

From The Charge of The Light Brigade By Alfred, Lord Tennyson

The precipitating event for the November, 1965 battle of Ia Drang Valley was the decision of Hanoi's military strategists to attempt to crush the ARVN under a powerful fall offensive.

The plan called for a full division of NVA regulars to penetrate the Central Highlands from the Ho Chi Minh trail, capture Pleiku city and control Route 19, all the way to the South China Sea. The theory was that whoever controls Route 19 also controls South Vietnam.

In retrospect, such ambitious goals for 1965-66 seem overly-simplistic and unrealistic. The United States knew of Hanoi's lofty ambitions for conquest and domination and had no intention of fiddling while Rome burned. On July 28, 1965, President Johnson announced to the nation during a morning address that he had ordered the Airmobile Division to Vietnam. The headquarters selected by the division, commonly known thereafter as the 1st Air Cavalry, was An Khe, half way up Route 19 on the road to Pleiku, the capital of the Central Highlands.

The stage was set. The United States and North Vietnam were each headed, in great strength, to the same place, but from opposite directions and on a clear collision course.

Harold G. Moore, Jr.

"I will leave no man behind...dead or alive. We will all come home together."
Hal Moore

Hal Moore, as he was content to be called, might have seemed at first blush too scholarly and unassuming to be handed the critical job of training and leading the vanguard air-ground assault against the NVA in the Central Highlands. But, Lt. Colonel Harold G. Moore, Jr., battle-tested in air assault operations as a paratrooper during the Korean War, combined the qualities of a soldier's soldier such as General Omar Bradley of World War II fame with great proficiency in mounting offensive operations against the enemy, reminiscent of General Matthew Ridgeway, the renowned Korean War Commanding General.

Thus, the Pentagon and Major General Henry Kinnard, the commanding officer of the army's newly-created Air Assault Test Division, were convinced they had the right man, when in April of 1964 they assigned Lt. Colonel Moore to command the 2nd Battalion, 23rd Infantry, which had been detached from the 2nd Infantry Division and assigned to the 11th Air Assault Test.

Without question, Hal Moore had an impressive curriculum vitae - West Point graduate, distinguished airborne combat soldier in Korea, graduate of the Command and General Staff College at Fort Leavenworth, service with the Pentagon Office of Research and Development, a tour of duty with NATO in Norway and a year of schooling at the Naval War College in Newport, Rhode Island. His academic credentials were further burnished by a Masters in International Relations from Harvard, leading some skeptics to comment that he was too bookish to be an effective field commander. As events would prove, they couldn't have been more wrong. In fact, it was both a gross insult and the height of the ridiculous to suggest that being well-educated and a great combat leader were mutually exclusive.

Lt. Colonel Hal Moore arrived at Fort Benning, Georgia, on June 27, 1964 and took command of his battalion on Monday, June 29th. In a brief address to his troops, Colonel Moore told them that the 2nd Battalion "was a good battalion but it would get better...I will do my best" he said; "I expect the same from each of you."[vi]

During the course of the hands-on training of the battalion, provided by Lt. Col. Moore and his staff, the troops soon learned that "doing their best" included learning each of their jobs from the man above them and then teaching it to the man below them. Moore knew that under his command the first man out of the assault helicopter at a hot landing zone (LZ) would likely be an officer or non-com, whether Squad Leader, Platoon Leader, Company Commander or Battalion Commander. If that man got hit, Moore expected the next in command behind him to immediately assume the downed Commander's duties, a seamless transfer of command so as to avoid delaying the disembarkation of the troops from the aircraft.

Moore's command was re-designated the 1st Battalion, 7th Air Cavalry. Perhaps not so coincidentally, the 7th Cavalry was also the last command of General George Armstrong Custer, an inspiring but chilling historical parallel. The battle cry of the men of the Air Cavalry was "Gary Owen" from the lilting tune of the same name which so inspired the horse cavalry of the early West.

Harold G. Moore Jr. was 42 years old when he arrived at Fort Benning, Georgia on June 27, 1964, accompanied by his wife and five growing children. As difficult as it was for him to leave his family in the summer of 1965 to lead his troops into a perilous campaign against the People's Army of North Vietnam, he did his best to explain to his children that while war was a terrible thing, he had to go in order to do his part in keeping his loved ones safe and free. His wife of many years, Julia Compton Moore, was also the daughter of an Army Colonel, and had always known that this type of heart-wrenching separation from her husband was part of being married to a professional soldier; and she faced it with equanimity. This fact, however, did not make it any less difficult to bear.

Once in-country the 1st Battalion settled in at the 1st Cavalry Division's base camp at An Khe, forty two miles west of the coastal city of Qui Non on Route 19.

When the strategically important city of Plei Me was attacked by the NVA in early November 1965, North Vietnam struck at the heart of the Central Highlands. Equally disturbing was the fact that they quickly retreated to a base camp on a mountain top near the Cambodian border.

It was as if they were daring the U.S. forces to come after them. Hal Moore and his 1st Battalion were handed the assignment of pursuing and destroying the NVA forces who had attacked Plei Mei and any others they could find. In the plus column, Moore had great confidence in the fighting spirit and skill of the men of the 1st Battalion, whom he had personally trained.

Basil L. Plumley

Fortunately for Moore, he was blessed with a resource of incalculable value in the battalion's Sergeant Major, Basil L. Plumley, a 44 year old battle scarred and grizzled warrior of singular distinction. Moore knew what he had in Plumley - a veteran of three wars who had parachuted into combat zones with the 82nd Airborne in World War II during the Allies' invasion of Sicily; again at Salerno, Italy; into Normandy on D Day; into Holland during Operation Market Garden and into Korea at the height of the war for control of that bloody peninsula.

Now Plumley was readying himself and his charges to confront the enemy once again in what would prove to be one of his bloodiest encounters ever. He was dead serious about the job that lay ahead and would brook no nonsense from the men, which included the young officers going into combat for the first time. But, he had the respect of the men and the full confidence of Colonel Moore, who in some ways relied on Plumley's judgment and operational skill, as if the latter were a co-commander. He was, in fact, Moore's adviser, confidant, alter-ego and loyal assistant. He had Moore's back and this probably saved the commander's life at Ia Drang.

Moore had no illusions about the operation which lay ahead. His battalion would spear-head an assault against an enemy the United States had never before fought, upon a terrain on which it had never set foot, with an under-strength battalion of only 395 men, pitted against a force of as many as 4000 NVA entrenched on a mountain top base camp.

He knew that many of his men would die during the engagement but he was determined to give them the best chance possible to survive.

In fact, the Air Cavalry did have some compensating advantages over the North Vietnamese - superior weaponry and firepower, greater mobility through the use of assault helicopters, better artillery and vastly superior air-power. If they were to survive, Moore would have to exploit these advantages to the hilt.

The first meeting in battle ever between the United States and North Vietnam began uneventfully enough on November 14, 1965 at 10:48 a.m. as a Huey helicopter piloted by an officer of exceptional skill, Major Bruce Crandall, touched down in a clearing in the dense forest and brush of the Ia Drang Valley. The first person to hit the ground when the helicopter landed was Lt. Colonel Harold G. Moore,

Jr., firing his M-16 in the direction of the tree line as soon as his feet hit the ground; and then running in the same direction he was firing. Immediately following Moore was Master Sergeant Basil L. Plumley and after him the other men on board the Huey who were also firing towards the edge of the clearing.

In the first wave, 16 Hueys deposited less than eighty men of the 1st Battalion at the LZ*, officially designated as LZ "X-ray".

When they had approached the clearing by air earlier, neither Moore nor Crandall saw any enemy troops on the ground; but Moore's instincts told him they weren't far away, and he was right. Of great concern to him was the fact that it would take the 16 Hueys under Major Crandall's command, about 30 minutes to get back to the base camp and return to the LZ with the second wave of soldiers. During that initial thirty minute period Moore would have less than eighty men on the ground to ward off an NVA attack, without even the help of helicopter gunners to lay suppressing fire on the approaching enemy. During that critical 30 minutes all the Hueys would be in use ferrying additional troops from the base camp to LZ X-ray. Hence, Moore's sense of urgency in driving off any NVA near the tree line, finding cover, establishing a perimeter and securing the LZ was acute. Compounding Moore's difficulties was the fact that the enemy was provided with excellent cover beyond the perimeter by 100 foot high trees and thick elephant grass.

A hot LZ would seriously endanger the landing of the Hueys and make it easier for the North Vietnamese to overrun the LZ and choke off the battalion's means of supply, reinforcement and escape.

The NVA were well-armed with weapons imported from the Soviet Union, China, Czechoslovakia and Albania, particularly the Kalashnikov AK-47 assault rifle. Their finely tuned intelligence network had fully prepared them for the American offensive. More than that, the NVA relished the idea of locking horns with the 1st Air Cavalry Division on the former's home turf, the dense overgrowth of the Ia Drang Valley near the Cambodian border and the Ho Chi Minh Trail.

North Vietnam was eager to engage the U.S. in major combat and considered themselves recipients of a great gift when Lt. Colonel Hal Moore's 1st Battalion, 7th Air Cavalry landed at LZ X-ray, smack in the middle of four NVA battalions of the 66th Regiment, totaling about 1,600 combat troops, plus one VC battalion.

*landing zone

The Ia Drang Valley was desolate. There were no villages, hooches, or civilians. Nevertheless, Moore, like General Custer at Little Bighorn eighty years earlier, was not deprived of a welcoming party. Within minutes after his touching down at X-ray, hundreds of NVA regulars began streaming down the side of Chu Pong Mountain from their base camp at the top, in the direction of the landing U.S. forces. Soon the greatly outnumbered American battalion and the confident NVA Regiment would be joined in a battle to the death.

Moore was not deceived by the uneventful landing at LZ X-ray. It was disquieting to him because, in his words, "Nothing was wrong except that nothing was wrong."[vii] He quickly dispatched patrols from Alpha Company into the woods beyond the western edge of the clearing, where there was a dry creek bed. To the south lay Chu Pong Mountain which Moore knew contained the NVA base camp.

In addition to sending a patrol into the woods west of the dry creek bed, Moore ordered Alpha Company to set up a defensive position in a cluster of trees near the creek bed.

The patrol soon captured an NVA soldier wandering alone in the woods and returned him to Moore's command post in a clump of trees on the northern edge of the clearing and east of the creek bed.

Under interrogation, the prisoner stated that there were three NVA battalions totaling about 1,600 combat troops who "want very much to kill Americans but had not been able to find any."[viii] As if to punctuate the point, gunfire broke out west of the dry creek bed.

Most of the 1st Battalion was now on the ground but Moore was quick to perceive the danger. He could not afford the luxury of sitting back and allowing the NVA with their vastly greater numbers to come to him. If that happened, the LZ would be overrun, choking off 1st Battalion from reinforcements, re-supply and a means of escape. No, Moore knew with a chilling certainty that either he attacked and engaged the enemy in battle in the woods west of the LZ and north of the NVA's mountain stronghold, or they would all die in the Ia Drang Valley.

First, as the remainder of 1st Battalion landed at approximately one-half hour intervals, Moore deployed them in such a manner as to establish a perimeter around the LZ. At the same time he dispatched Bravo Company under the command of Captain John Herren, another calm, cool and intelligent leader, to penetrate the woods in full force to the west and south of the dry creek bed, in order to interdict the waves of NVA rapidly moving down the mountainside. Herren's job was to aggressively engage the NVA in battle in the woods while Moore called artillery strikes in on them. The American artillery position had been established a few miles to the northeast of the LZ.

Soon a fierce and bloody firefight was underway in the woods between Bravo Company and NVA troops arriving in force from their mountain redoubt.

The gravity and urgency of his situation was not lost on Lt. Col. Moore. His self-evaluation in his own words was as follows:

"Only if we brought the enemy to battle deep in the trees and brush would we stand even a slim chance of holding on to the clearing and getting the rest of the battalion landed. That football field-size clearing was our lifeline and our supply line. If the enemy closed the way to the helicopters all of us would die in that place."[ix]

What Moore didn't seem to fully grasp was that if he himself died, the battalion, bereft of his leadership, would likely crumble. His regimental commander, Colonel Tim Brown, had given both Moore and Plumley a somewhat unorthodox warning on the night before the battle to take special care of themselves. This would appear to have been less premonition than a hard-headed appeal to caution, born of a knowledge of what they would be up against. Yet, as the NVA probed and attacked the perimeters of X-ray, firing and lobbing mortars and grenades into the clearing, Moore stood at his full height in the open, shouting orders to his troops. Plumley was aghast at Moore's apparent obliviousness to the degree to which he was placing himself at risk, and implored Moore to get down and take cover. He finally convinced the battalion commander to get out of the clear line of fire, by shouting at him that if he got killed, they would likely all fall in the impending NVA onslaught.

Meanwhile, Herren's Bravo Company was involved in a fierce fire fight west of the dry creek bed and was taking casualties. Herren's left flank was protected by Alpha Company but his right flank was exposed. Moore had admonished Herren not to let his company be outflanked at the creek bed. So, when the NVA forces attempted to outflank Bravo Company on its right flank, Herren radioed 2nd Lt. Henry Herrick to lead his 2nd Platoon around to the right and to hook up with and reinforce the platoon in danger on Bravo Company's right flank.

Herrick did proceed to make contact with Bravo's right flank but, amazingly kept right on going until his 2nd Platoon was deep in the woods and far ahead of the rest of the battalion. He soon found himself cut off and surrounded by the NVA at a small knoll perhaps several hundred yards northwest of LZ - X-ray. For the remainder of the day as the battle raged, Moore sent elements of 1st Battalion to attempt to hook up with Herrick's 2nd Platoon and rescue them. None of the attempts were successful as the heavy concentration of NVA surrounding Herrick proved deadly and impenetrable.

There could be no questioning the bravery and dedication of 2nd Lt. Herrick but his lightning thrust past Bravo's right flank was a foolish move which led to the loss of most of his platoon and the loss of his own life. But, 2" Platoon, despite staggering losses, fought on with tenacity from their isolated position at the slightly elevated knoll.

Ironically, Herrick's action confused the NVA into thinking that U.S. forces had established a much wider and deeper presence in the areas around the LZ, in far greater numbers than they actually had, prompting the NVA to allocate disproportionate numbers of troops near and around the knoll. This had the effect of diluting the concentrated strength of the NVA overall offensive, and contributing to the eventual U.S. victory. Even though it wasn't planned that way, Herrick's rash action had the effect of a ruse, which completely fooled the NVA.

On November 14, 1965, however, the fierceness of the NVA attack combined with Moore's call for airpower to level some trees to the northeast of X-ray so that a secondary LZ could be established at a smaller clearing, plus the lost 2nd Platoon, gave division command at An Khe a skewed take on how the battle was progressing. Things were actually more positive than they seemed and as Moore and Plumley walked the entire perimeter that evening, they were heartened by the fact that 1st Battalion was holding at all critical points. Moore and Plumley found the troops battered and saddened by the loss of their comrades during the day's combat, but their morale was good. The upbeat demeanor of Moore and Plumley buoyed their spirits as they prepared mentally and physically for the all-out enemy onslaught expected in the morning.

The battle was only one day old but the American losses had already been devastating.

Lieutenant Robert E. Taft, the platoon leader of 3rd Platoon, Alpha Company, died when he was shot in the throat as he led his greatly outnumbered platoon against a force of 150 NVA charging at them on both sides of the creek bed. Russell Adams, a short-timer with only 14 days to go in his Vietnam tour and an M-60 gunner with 3" Platoon, and Bill Beck, his fellow machine gunner, charged far ahead of the rest of the platoon, all the while pouring machine gun fire into the tightly-grouped enemy, from their weapons held at their sides. The heavy casualties inflicted upon the NVA by the courageous machine gunners probably saved Alpha Company's left flank but couldn't save Sergeant Alexander Williams from taking a bullet in his forehead, killing him instantly. Also killed in the skirmish at the creek bed were Sergeant Travis Poss and Specialist 4, Albert Witcher. The air-cavalrymen, however, gave as good as they got and the NVA losses the first day of the battle were far worse than those suffered by Colonel Moore's battalion.

Walter J. Marm

Lt. Walter J. (Joe) Marm's platoon collided with a heavy force of NVA troopers as the latter drifted to their right after unsuccessfully attempting to flank Bravo Company. Marm's platoon mowed them down with a withering barrage of machine gun and rifle fire. During the firefight Lieutenant Marm caught sight of an enemy machine gun emplacement dug into an anthill, delivering a deadly barrage of fire into the midst of the prone soldiers of two Bravo platoons. A tossed grenade and a U.S. rocket had failed to neutralize the NVA machine gun, so Marm decided to take matters into his own hands. He sprang to his feet, charged the machine gun position and tossed a hand grenade behind the anthill, taking out an NVA officer and twelve enemy soldiers. Marm had saved the lives of many and in doing so took a bullet in his neck and jaw. But, he survived his wound, was evacuated and within a few days was recuperating in Valley Forge Army Hospital, not far from his Pennsylvania home.

Marm had repeatedly placed himself in harm's way as he led his platoon and was the only ground soldier to receive the Medal of Honor for valor in the Ia Drang Campaign.

When one considers the heroic acts of men like Geoghegan, Herren, Savage, Adams and Beck during the Battle of Ia Drang Valley, it is surprising that more Medal of Honor recipients were not named for the extraordinary conduct they displayed during the two day encounter. But, the military's system for awarding honors for conduct above and beyond the call of duty is not perfect. There are too many separate actions and statements that have to be made by too many diverse people - witnesses, field commanders, headquarters commanders, Pentagon officials, etc.; and too many exercises of individual judgment and discretion that have to be made in deciding who is decorated and at what level, for the system to be without serious flaws. Circumstances and luck are major parts of the equation. Many worthy candidates who deserve the Medal of Honor have not received it. Fortunately, the reverse is not true. Very few, if any, of the individuals who have received the Medal of Honor were undeserving of the award.

Calvin Bouknight

In the meantime as the NVA infiltrated between Herrick's isolated platoon and the rest of Bravo, Specialist 5 Calvin Bouknight, a medic, abandoned his position of cover and ran into the line of fire to treat wounded men lying on the ground. By putting his body between the enemy fire and the man he was treating, Bouknight was successful in treating 4 or 5 of the wounded. Twenty four year old Calvin Bouknight's heroism probably saved their lives, but in so doing, he himself was mortally wounded, when an enemy round caught him right between the shoulders. Bouknight knew he was dying as he lay on the ground after his comrades had with great care placed him there in his rubber poncho. Like so many other heroes, his life and death reached a crescendo of bravery and selflessness within a matter of minutes, not hours, days or years, as if encapsulated in a few cinematic freeze frames.

Bouknight died the way he had lived his short life - with simple dignity but uncommon valor. As he reached up and took the hand of his close friend, Sergeant First Class Thomas Keeton, his laconic pronouncement was a simple, "Sarge I didn't make it."[x]

The Lost Platoon

At the knoll, Herrick's platoon was surrounded and under assault from the north, south and east by 150 NVA soldiers. Herrick was making a courageous and effective stand but his platoon was, little by little, being decimated in a hail of enemy fire. His machine gun position was overrun and Herrick himself took a bullet in the hip. Seconds before he went into shock, Herrick told one of his comrades, "If I have to die, I'm glad to give my life for my country."[x] Herrick died minutes later, lying on the ground behind the low ridge of the knoll next to a small pile of brush.

Sergeant Carl A. Palmer, two days shy of his 40th birthday, took over command of the platoon but he too was killed when a grenade exploded behind him. Before the battle, the experienced and highly capable Palmer had predicted he would not live to see his 40th birthday. His prediction turned out to be grimly prophetic. Sergeant Robert L. Stokes, age 24, succeeded Sergeant Palmer but was shot twice in the head shortly thereafter and became the 3rd Platoon leader killed at the knoll. Command had passed from Herrick to Palmer to Stokes and finally to buck sergeant, Ernie Savage. Savage, despite his relatively low rank and lack of command experience, did an exemplary job. He skillfully called in artillery fire upon the attacking NVA while directing the defense of the U.S. position. The remaining fighters, about 12 in number, retrieved the ammo of their dead comrades and fought for their lives, determined to hold their position until the end.

Day Two

The lost platoon survived through the night and as darkness yielded first light to dawn, Moore ruminated over new ways to rescue them. As it happened, he soon had the even more pressing problem of fashioning the survival of a battalion. His patrols probed the foreboding sylvan density beyond X-ray's perimeter and soon scurried back to shout that they had found the enemy and it was headed right for the south and southeast perimeter in great numbers.

Moore's Command Post was on the northern side of the clearing opposite the main point of attack. Enemy AK 47 fire intended for the southern perimeter zinged across the clearing, past the ears of Moore, Plumley and other C.P. personnel.

Charlie Company was initially taking the brunt of the attack as it fought off two or three companies of NVA. Lieutenants Geoghegan and Kroger commanded the platoons in the biggest trouble. Lieutenant Geoghegan eventually died in defense of the perimeter. The enemy attackers had managed to infiltrate the lines and creep in around the platoons' flanks. The seemingly invincible perimeter had been breached, shattering the illusion that the U.S. defenses would remain inviolate throughout the battle.

In their fox holes, approximately ten feet apart, the two imperiled platoons fought for their lives. Only the non-stop blizzard of lead from his platoon's M-60 machine guns was keeping Geoghegan's platoon from being overrun by scores of NVA, cleverly camouflaged with branches stuck in the webbing of their helmets, to give them the momentary appearance of trees. The attack upon Charlie Company came so fast and furious that Company Commander Bob Edwards did not have enough time to call in artillery fire on the attacking NVA before they were on top of the U.S. defenders. Edwards was hit in the left shoulder, began bleeding profusely from his wound and his left arm was soon useless.

Charlie Company's situation was so dire that the code-word "broken arrow" was radioed out. The translation was "American unit in contact and in danger of being overrun." Soon U.S. aircraft from all parts of South Vietnam were raining down their ordnance, including napalm, on the NVA positions.

By 7:15 a.m. a second heavy NVA assault was launched against Delta Company at the eastern portion of the perimeter.

Alpha Company left its platoons to the right of Charlie Company's right flank in place to prevent it from collapsing, but quickly sent another of its platoons to the aid of the imperiled Lieutenant Neil Kroger and the men of Delta Company. At the same time, Lieutenant Geoghegan's platoon was also in deep trouble and on the verge of collapse. Chaos was everywhere throughout the LZ as Master Sergeant Plumley standing straight up, moved from the point of attack to the Battalion Aid Station and boomed in the direction of the doctor and medics, "Gentlemen, prepare to defend yourselves."[xi]

As enemy fire seemed to be everywhere and coming from all directions. Lieutenant Colonel Moore still commanded a small reserve in the center of the clearing. The NVA was attacking from the southeast and northwest while the VC attacked from the southwest.

The threat of a break-through of the entire U.S. perimeter was real and imminent. But, soon after Colonel Moore shouted "Broken Arrow, Broken Arrow" into the radio there commenced a ferocious pounding of the North Vietnamese and VC from the air causing the NVA attack in the North to stall.

In the South, however, the situation was critical. The defenders from Charlie and Delta Companies had been pushed back off the perimeter, and the command post itself, under heavy fire, was in danger of being overrun. But suddenly, life imitated art, Hollywood-style. Moore got the happy news that more cavalry was on the way to relieve the battered outpost. 2nd Battalion was in the air in Major Bruce Crandall's Hueys and would soon be landing. Still, Moore knew that desperate measures were called for to both ease the crisis and to allow 2nd Battalion to land. It was time to counter attack!

The VC had taken control of the tree-line in the Southwest and were confidently pouring fire into the LZ. It would only be a matter of time before the U.S. perimeter would collapse entirely. The Vietnamese were feeling pretty confident about ultimate victory and their mood was self-congratulatory. The Americans were back on their heels and the NVA/VC force could smell victory. Their shock and surprise, therefore, was total when without warning Alpha Company boldly charged across the LZ in an all-out attack upon the VC battalion at the southwest tree-line. The U.S. attack was as dangerous as it was gutsy, but it worked. Taking full advantage of the element of surprise, Alpha Company practically routed the stunned VC just as the Hueys carrying 2nd Battalion zoomed over the tree tops above them.

2nd Battalion landed in the hottest LZ they had ever seen and were engaged in a fire-fight immediately upon landing. But, greatly helped by 2nd Battalion's reinforcement of 1st Battalion's battered troops, the tide began to change and the NVA attack was repelled. Colonel Moore's fighting First Battalion had so many dead and wounded that they were evacuated on the following day, November 16, 1965. They had bent but they never broke and they were even successful in rescuing the lost platoon on the third try. So brutal was the fighting that when the smoke had cleared, near the perimeter was a dead U.S. soldier in a fox hole surrounded by 5 dead NVA soldiers. Another dead U.S. trooper was found with his hands locked around the neck of a dead NVA soldier.*

The epic battle at LZ X-ray was over but another began on November 16th at LZ Albany. The battles in the Ia Drang Valley demonstrated the awesome fire power which the U.S. could mount in overcoming a numerical disadvantage in any given battle. They also demonstrated the skill and bravery of the American fighting men who theretofore were considered by Hanoi to be too slow, too immobile and too predictable. North Vietnam and the leaders of the Viet Cong learned that it was nothing short of folly to repeatedly engage the highly mobile and powerful air cavalry in direct and open warfare. Guerrilla warfare and close-in combat against the U.S. forces would prove to be far more effective.

Overall, 234 Americans died at the Battle of Ia Drang and 242 were wounded, as compared to approximately 1037 NVA killed and 1365 wounded.

---

*See endnote number "xiii" for citation to Eyewitness Vietnam (at page 117)

As bloody and costly as the battle was, it buoyed the morale of U.S. forces in Vietnam. Ultimately, it had come down to Lieutenant Colonel Moore's dogma of each man looking out for the next, as the men of 1st Battalion fought first and foremost for each other.

Harold Moore led elements of the 7th Cavalry into battle against the Vietnamese for 235 more days, but the battle in the Ia Drang Valley on November 14th through 16th was for him, without question, the most dramatic, memorable and emotionally jarring. The incredible performance of he and his men under some of the most harrowing conditions imaginable vindicated the soundness of the lessons he had taught them: team work, togetherness and unconditional devotion to their unit and each other. In addressing his officers and noncoms before the Battle of Ia Drang, Moore passionately told them: "Take care of your men. All we'll have is each other."

The names of the soldiers of the 7th Cavalry who died in the Battle of Ia Drang Valley are carved into Panel 3 East of the Vietnam Memorial, in Washington, D.C.

Edward W. Freeman

The effort of the Army Air Cavalry at Ia Drang succeeded in no small measure due to the gallantry, skill and experience of a cadre of battle-tested veterans such as Hal Moore, Basil Plumley and Bruce Crandall. Captain Edward W. Freeman also belongs in their august company. An experienced combat vet who earned a battlefield commission in Korea, Freeman was second in command to Crandall of the 16-helicopter unit which deposited Moore and his first battalion at LZ X-ray on November 14, 1965, and rescued, reinforced and re-supplied them thereafter.

As the battle raged on day 1, the battalion found itself almost out of ammunition. Things couldn't have looked any bleaker. Lieutenant Colonel Moore had been forced to close the landing zone in the face of withering enemy fire. This didn't stop Freeman, however, as he repeatedly risked his own life by weaving his unarmed helicopter through a blizzard of enemy fire, time and time again, and landing in the midst of intense enemy fire and exploding grenades and mortars, to deliver fresh ammunition, water and medical supplies to the embattled inhabitants of LZ X-ray.

Later, when medevac helicopters refused to fly into the area because of the unremitting NVA fire, Freeman again risked his life by flying fourteen separate rescue missions and evacuating thirty seriously wounded soldiers, many of whom owed him their lives.

All of Freeman's landings were made in the small emergency zone Moore had established when X-ray got too hot, 100 to 200 meters from the imperiled LZ. For his exceptional bravery in placing himself in harm's way over and over again to save American lives, Edward W. Freeman was the deserving recipient of the Medal of Honor.

The Iron Triangle

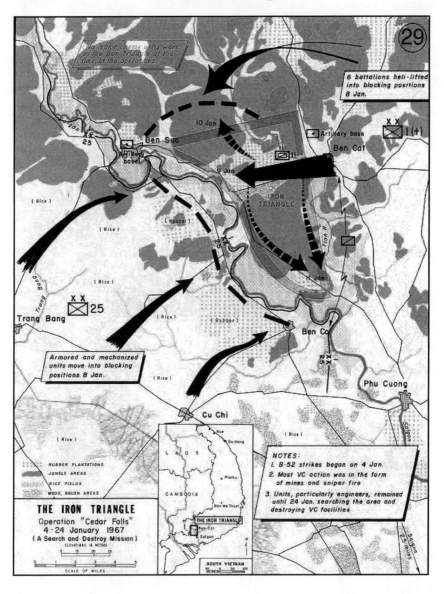

No major enemy units were in the Iron Triangle at the time of the operations.

6 battalions heli-lifted into blocking positions 8 Jan.

Artillery base

Ben Cat

XX
25

Artillery base

Ben Suc

10 Jan

III
II

9 Jan

IRON TRIANGLE

Trinh R.

(Rice)

(Rubber)

(Rice)

XX
25

(Rice)

Trang Bang

(Rice)

(Rubber)

Ben Co

Armored and mechanized units move into blocking positions 8 Jan.

(Rice)

XX
25

Phu Cuong

Cu Chi

(Rice)

(Rice)

NOTES:
1. B-52 strikes began on 4 Jan.
2. Most VC action was in the form of mines and sniper fire
3. Units, particularly engineers, remained until 24 Jan. searching the area and destroying VC facilities

RUBBER PLANTATIONS
JUNGLE AREAS
RICE FIELDS
WOOD, BRUSH AREAS

THE IRON TRIANGLE
Operation "Cedar Falls"
4-24 January 1967
(A Search and Destroy Mission)
ELEVATIONS IN METERS

SCALE OF MILES

Hue
Da Nang

LAOS

Pleiku

CAMBODIA

Ban Me Thuot

THE IRON TRIANGLE
Ben Cat
Saigon

SOUTH VIETNAM

Saigon
25 miles

CHAPTER V
The Iron Triangle: 1966

Encouraged by the Seventh Air Cavalry success in the Ia Drang Valley, General Westmoreland initiated a series of search and destroy operations in January of 1966 with the aim of dealing a knock-out punch to the NVA and VC.

U.S. troops in South Vietnam at that point numbered close to two hundred thousand and the U.S. military command was optimistic about their prospects of scoring a major, if not decisive, U.S. victory.

1. Operation Cedar Falls

The area Northeast and Northwest of Saigon, dubbed "The Iron Triangle" ranged from being an annoyance at certain times to a menace at others, to the capital city, the ARVN and U.S. Forces and Installations. Beneath The Iron Triangle lay an elaborate system of Viet Cong tunnels from which they could mount and support operations and then disappear after an attack.

Of all targets General Westmoreland wanted to search and destroy, the intricate VC tunnel system was at the top of the list. A "clearing operation" was initiated by U.S. forces on January 8, 1966 as three full Army divisions under the command of General Jonathan 0. Seaman moved into The Iron Triangle, forty square miles of jungle and thick growth. The offensive was called Operation Cedar Falls.

Westmoreland's decision was hardly misdirected. The Iron Triangle was the Viet Cong base of operations and its nerve center.From there it could control the surrounding roads, bridges, rivers and other infrastructure, enabling it to threaten Saigon almost with impunity. The Viet Cong could mount an attack on the capital and then retreat, if necessary, into an underground sanctuary.

Before the U.S. operation commenced, the entire forty square miles was sprayed with Agent Orange, a chemical defoliant, to clear the thick jungle growth and allow U.S. forces to move through the area without major obstructions in their way.

After the war ended, Agent Orange became a notorious term since the chemicals were believed to contain carcinogens, including dioxin and to have caused cancer in hundreds of Vietnam vets. Controversy and litigation raged for years and the issue has never been satisfactorily resolved, another frightening legacy of the war, bequeathed to American veterans and their families.

Early in the operation, elements under the command of General Alexander D Haig, a future U.S. Secretary of State, located the main tunnel system. Specially trained GI's called "Tunnel Rats" crawled into the vast complex of tunnels in pursuit of Viet Cong. They were armed principally with flashlights and nerves of steel. These men were strictly volunteers and no one with a history of claustrophobia applied for the job.

2. The Tunnel Rats

The underground complexes beneath The Iron Triangle were called the CuChi tunnels. An American combat soldier who volunteered for and was accepted as a "Tunnel Rat" was truly a breed apart. It took some kind of guts and nerve to crawl into a hole in the ground that might be mined or booby trapped to pursue an enemy who was in all likelihood lying in wait to kill you.

An American Tunnel Rat had to know that if he encountered a VC soldier somewhere in the Byzantine complex beneath the ground, the VC would have the distinct advantage of fighting in his own habitat. The odds of the U.S. soldier killing his enemy counterpart before the enemy killed him were not very good.

The Tunnel Rat, usually slight of build and short in stature, entered the labyrinth equipped with only a semiautomatic M1911 handgun and a flashlight. The blasts from the handgun in a confined subterranean space were frequently so deafening that the Tunnel Rat was left temporarily deaf.[xii] If he could get his hands on a German Luger or Walther pistol, with a quieter discharge, he could probably retain his hearing.

The multiple dangers presented by the tunnels were beyond predicting or safeguarding against. The Tunnel Rat was alone, isolated and often incommunicado. He had nothing but his own thoughts and fears for company. Up ahead he might encounter trapped, deadly gas. There were holes in the walls of the tunnels through which the VC could thrust a spear, impaling him and converting the tunnel into the soldier's grave. Or, the VC might flood the tunnel and drown him; or explode it and obliterate him. And, if the VC didn't get the Tunnel Rat, he could still be victimized by any number of non-human species such as snakes, scorpions, rats and bats. After completing their tours of duty in Vietnam, the Tunnel Rats frequently suffered from some of the worst forms of post-traumatic stress syndrome known to man. The stress they experienced was unprecedented and at times unbearable - many returned from Vietnam as haunted men.

It was amazing that the U.S. military was able to get any volunteers at all. But, they did and the Tunnel Rats played a significant role in purging the CuChi tunnels of approximately 1000 VC during Operation Cedar Falls.

When all was said and done, however, Operation Cedar Falls was only partially successful. Possessed of good advance intelligence from their network of spies, most of the VC fled The Iron Triangle and the tunnels before the Americans arrived. The Americans attempted to destroy the tunnel complex with explosives, but many of the tunnels survived and remained intact. Shortly after Operation Cedar Falls was completed the VC were back in The Iron Triangle and in the tunnels in great numbers. Two years later The Iron Triangle was one of the main staging areas for the Tet offensive, as the Viet Cong streamed out the tunnels and attacked Saigon.

The CuChi tunnels have survived until the present day and are now a popular tourist attraction. For a reasonable fee, a tour guide, perhaps a former Viet Cong soldier himself, will accompany an interested tourist on a guided tour into the tunnels.

Nevertheless, the Tunnel Rats were special U.S. heroes whose exploits during the Vietnam War went largely unnoticed and under appreciated. They should have been placed on the same pedestal with the Army Rangers, the Green Berets, the Navy Seals, the Marine Infantry and all of the other more celebrated combat fighters.

The dark, dangerous and depressing work of the Tunnel Rats did not lend itself to the creation of an heroic prototype. For that matter, the Vietnam War, in general, has not been celebrated by America either. Forty years later it still evokes controversy and bitter disagreements. The Hollywood depictions of the war in classic films such as <u>Apocalypse Now</u>, <u>Platoon</u> and <u>Full Metal Jacket</u>, have portrayed it as a dark and foreboding exercise in moral ambiguity, sometimes bordering on a hellish insanity. This is not all bad. The glorification of World War II in novels, plays, movies and television shows was over-the-top and probably gave the youth of America who grew up in its aftermath a skewed, distorted and overly romantic view of war.

Those of us who came of age during the Vietnam era are still waiting for history to place the cataclysm which was the Vietnam War in its proper historical perspective.

3. America's Flying Warriors

United States air power was so praised for its impact in the Vietnam War that one could almost imagine this force as a powerful entity unto itself and lose sight of the fact that it was composed of thousands of brave and skilled pilots and crew members, both in the air and on the ground. The main aircraft employed against the Viet Cong and North Vietnam were the helicopter, the strike plane piloted by a fighter pilot and usually armed with bombs, the B-52 bomber, the F-105 Weasel which was an anti-surface to air missile plane tasked with protecting the fighter planes from S.A.M. missiles and the F-104 also known as a MIG-Cap whose function was to protect the Weasels by keeping North Vietnamese MIGS away from them. The U.S. had the most advanced planes and the best pilots in the World. It was no accident that the ARVN only fell to the North Vietnamese forces after American air power was withdrawn from the conflict.

Leo K. Thorsness

Lieutenant Colonel Leo K. Thorsness of the United States Air Force was a flyboy through and through. Whether he immersed himself in the pilot's culture of heavy off-duty partying is not common knowledge but he certainly shared the elan and daring that seemed to be prerequisites for being a fighter jock. He also had that special ability prominently mentioned in Tom Wolf's The Right Stuff of being able to "maintain an even strain" at all times.

Thorsness was a staunch Midwesterner, born in 1932 in Walnut Grove, Minnesota. He enlisted in the Air Force in 1952 at age 19 because he had a brother serving in Korea. But, even though he enlisted at an early age, he still managed to get a good education, receiving a bachelor's degree from the University of Omaha and a master's degree from the University of Southern California. In 1966, he got his orders for Vietnam - to fly F-105 Weasels with the mission to destroy North Vietnamese SAMs (surface to air missiles).

On April 19, 1966, Lt. Col. Thorsness and his wingman destroyed a SAM with an air to ground missile. Then they knocked out a second SAM site with bombs. But, things were going too well. As they were reveling in their success, anti-aircraft fire squarely hit the wingman's plane. The plane went down and its two occupants parachuted out. Thorsness's F-105 was low on fuel but that fact had no influence on his next action, which was to head in the direction of the downed crew members' position on the ground, in order to rescue them. Being low on fuel wasn't Thorsness's only problem. As he headed towards his wingman's location he came under a barrage of heavy SAM and anti-aircraft fire. On top of that he was forced to drive away four North Vietnamese MIGS from the rescue area.

Thorsness's day's work wasn't over yet. Before returning to base he directed and accompanied another low on fuel plane to a recovery base where it could safely re-fuel.

In addition to receiving the Medal of Honor for his actions on April 19, 1966, Thorsness also ultimately received the Silver Star, the Distinguished Flying Cross and the Purple Heart.

Two weeks after his extraordinary feat, while flying his 93rd mission, only three missions shy of completing his tour, Lt. Col. Leo Thorsness was shot down over North Vietnam. Thorsness and his other crew member, backseater Capt. Harold Johnson, ejected from the plane and parachuted into enemy territory where they were captured. Imprisoned in the infamous "Hanoi Hilton", Thorsness resisted his captors' demands and spent a year in solitary confinement for refusal to cooperate. He was also subjected to torture, resulting in serious back injuries. He spent six years in captivity. While imprisoned, Thorsness was awarded the Medal of Honor but it was not announced until after he was released in 1973, primarily so that his captors would not hold it against him and subject him to more severe punishment. Not all American POWs were as tough as Thorsness. As in all wars, a certain percentage of captives cracked under the strain and provided their captors with information on their fellow POWs and sometimes on U.S. operational plans. The U.S. military hiearchy could not know with any certainty who was cooperating with the enemy and who wasn't. Hence, the Pentagon was inclined to withold high honors until after the serviceman was released, lest it suffer the great embarrassment of honoring a man unworthy of the honor.

Lt. Col. Thorsness survived his injuries and captivity and after retirement from the Air Force was ultimately elected to the Washington State Senate, where he was able to continue his life long effort to serve the public.

Chapter VI
The Pivotal Year, 1968

1. The Tet Offensive

The most historically significant military engagement of the Vietnam War was the Tet offensive, which began on January 30, 1968. The coordinated NVA and VC attacks upon 35 cities simultaneously throughout South Vietnam caught U.S. forces under the command of General William C. Westmoreland, as well as the ARVN, by complete surprise.

The offensive led by the legendary North Vietnamese general, Vo Nguyen Giap, the hero of Dien Bien Phu, was brilliantly conceived, both militarily and psychologically. For months the NVA and VC had been moving men and material to strategic points of attack throughout the Republic of South Vietnam, without being detected by ARVN intelligence or the vaunted intelligence services of the United States. The timing of the invasions was ingenious - they began during the Vietnamese lunar New Year celebration when most ARVN soldiers had returned to their home towns or regions on leave, to partake of the nation-wide celebration.

Although the offensive was turned back by combined U.S. and ARVN forces in most areas of the country, while inflicting tremendous casualties upon the attackers, the embarrassment and psychological damage suffered by the United States was incalculable. Since 1965, President Johnson,

Secretary of Defense McNamara, General Westmoreland and other high U.S. officials had been publicly dismissive about the strength and capabilities of the NVA and VC, almost to the point of contempt. The people of America and allied nations had been assured repeatedly that the enemy forces were back on their heals, were not an effective fighting force capable of mounting a serious challenge to the United States and its allies and that the U.S. was winning the war.

Such complacency and arrogance only compounded the severe shock felt throughout the United States and among its fighting men and women, when they learned that NVA and VC commandos as well as conventional forces, had slipped past and through the formidable U.S. and ARVN defenses and infiltrated into most major South Vietnamese cities. There they proceeded to attack lightly guarded government buildings, embassies and military headquarters, before being detected.

In Saigon on January 31, 1968 at 3:00 a.m. 19 VC commandos wearing red bandanas on their heads smashed through the wall of the U.S. Embassy onto the embassy grounds upon receiving the signal from their commander in civilian clothes, who was driving through the main streets of Saigon in a black Citroen. Upon his command, the VC also hit other targets throughout the city at approximately the same time. Altogether six cities were hit simultaneously at or about 3:00 a.m., spreading panic and confusion throughout the country. By the end of the day some eighty thousand VC and NVA soldiers had begun an assault on more than forty South Vietnamese cities and towns.

Among the largest cities hit were Saigon, Quang Tri, Da Nang and Hué.

Most of the attacks were driven back and the ratio of VC and NVA killed to those of the U.S. military and the ARVN was overwhelmingly in favor of the U.S. and South Vietnam. The opposite was true when it came to the psychological damage. The American public were nothing short of astounded. That General Giap could have caught the mighty American forces in such a state of somnolence everywhere, exposed the hollowness of U.S. boasts and did permanent damage to its credibility.

Spurred on by the national and international media, a strong anti-war movement gathered steam in the United States, eventually leading to the withdrawal of Lyndon Johnson from political life, the election of Richard Nixon as United States President, the removal of U.S. combat troops from Vietnam in 1973 and the fall of the Republic of Vietnam in 1975.

None of this, however, diminished the valor and skill of the American forces on the ground, in the air and at sea. Heavy fighting continued for months afterward at Hué, Khe Sanh, the A Shau Valley and elsewhere. In these battles the American soldiers, sailors, airmen and marines acquitted themselves brilliantly and heroically. The U.S. won a decisive military victory during Tet, killing as many as 40,000 VC regular soldiers[xiii] but suffered a psychological defeat which had a far longer-lasting impact, as American public opinion steadily turned against the war. The Tet offensive was a military failure for the NVA and VC. Success was to have been predicated upon two key factors, the element of surprise and an internal uprising by the South Vietnamese people against the existing government in Saigon. The second element, an expected grass roots revolt, simply never happened. The first element, surprise, led to some instances of early success, but poor execution by the combined NVA and VC forces and a ferocious counter-attack by the U.S. and ARVN, evicted the NVA and VC from whatever real estate they initially seized.

Nevertheless, the blood bath did not spare either side and devastated both combatants and non-combatants alike. As an example, large numbers of VC political cadre were wiped out by the allied forces during the counter-offensive into what had theretofore been VC strongholds; while in Hué, almost 6000 civilians loyal to the South Vietnamese government were slaughtered by the NVA and VC, many of them buried alive. The NVA and VC murdered a thousand government workers at ARVN headquarters alone

Taken in its larger context, the Tet Offensive was the pivotal event of the Vietnam War. If the VC and NVA could attack in massive numbers any time and at any place, what had the mighty U.S. forces been doing for the last three years to secure the safety and stability of South Vietnam? A parallel to the widespread skepticism in the wake of the Tet offensive is present in the questions now being asked about the U.S. military involvement in Iraq.

The collective American psyche never really recovered from the trauma of Tet and thereafter neither the politicians nor the generals were able to muster the public support necessary to see the war effort through to a successful conclusion.

Drew D. Dix

Some of the most conspicuous acts of American gallantry during Tet, or for that matter during the entire war, were performed by individual U.S. soldiers serving as advisers to ARVN units, under the umbrella of the U.S. Military Assistance Command Vietnam (MACV). The very conditions under which they served seemed to create opportunities for extraordinary valor. For one thing, the American advisers usually were looked to for leadership by the ARVN units to which they were assigned. For another, when sudden hostilities broke out, as they did during the Tet offensive, the individual U.S. adviser was often geographically remote from his command and support structure and was forced to either seize the command initiative or perish. Very often he was the only person attached to the unit with the combat training and experience necessary for leadership.

Such an American was Staff Sergeant Drew D. Dix, a 23 year old military adviser in the mountainous region of the Mekong Delta named Chau Doc Province. Situated near the Cambodian border and not far from the Ho Chi Minh Trail, Chau Doc Province was a relatively easy target for the NVA and VC. It was, therefore, thrown immediately into crisis mode when well-equipped VC battalions poured across the nearby Cambodian border and into Chau Doc in the early hours of January 31, 1968.

Born on December 14, 1944 at West Point, New York, Sergeant Drew D. Dix worked long and hard as an Army enlistee to attain his M.O.S.[XIV] as a counter-terrorism specialist. Admired for his thorough professionalism and unflagging dedication to whatever task was placed before him, he gained a reputation in Vietnam as a "soldier's soldier". It came as no surprise to his admirers when he received a prestigious assignment to U.S. Senior Adviser Group, IV Corp., Military Assistance Command, as a unit adviser in Chau Phu, the capital of Chau Doc Province.

As synchronized attacks began on January 31, 1968 in the early morning darkness against carefully selected targets having strategic or symbolic value in Saigon and elsewhere, NVA and VC forces near Chau Doc Province were on the cusp of a major assault and hopefully from their standpoint, a takeover of Chau Phu.

When the balloon went up on the morning of January 31, 1968 as part of the Tet Offensive, two well-armed VC battalions smashed into Chau Phu. The defenses of the city, in a state of unpreparedness, were quickly penetrated and overwhelmed. Sergeant Dix, however, in command of an ARVN unit, mobilized his men quickly and moved to successfully perform his first task, the rescue of a nurse trapped by the vanguard elements of the enemy attack.

Dix followed that mission of mercy by rescuing eight more civilians trapped within Chau Phu in a building under heavy VC mortar and small arms fire.

Having dispatched the rescue missions quickly, Dix and his unit headed for the center of the city to combat the VC invaders in earnest. Near central Chau Phu, Dix and his men were suddenly hit by heavy automatic machine gun and rifle fire from a building under VC control. It was impossible to know at that point how many VC lay within the walls of the building, but heedless of personal risk, Dix bravely charged into the enemy stronghold, personally killing six VC and rescuing two Filipinos. Within the first hour of fighting Dix had rescued eleven civilians.

On the first day of the assault upon Chau Phu, the VC had made significant inroads, but Dix's unit had only begun their counter-offensive. He was virtually isolated from any command guidance and free to seize the initiative on his own. Hence, on the second day he busied himself assembling a 20 man attack force. As soon as his charges were briefed and battle-ready, Dix led a charge upon the VC -occupied hotel, theater and adjacent buildings.[xv] The return fire from the VC, sequestered behind the buildings' walls, slashed into the attacking South Vietnam fighters led by Sergeant Dix, with an unforgiving ferocity. But, notwithstanding the enemy fire, Dix's raiders were successful in clearing the VC out of the inhabited buildings.

Dix also led by example. The sometimes timid ARVN units of Chau Phu, now inspired by Dix's audacious attacks against the VC invaders, rallied strongly. Perhaps they were not about to let an American soldier display more courage and tenacity in the defense of their homeland than they themselves did. Whatever the reason, they soon took up the cause with a vengeance, taking on the VC, who were now on the defensive, head on.

In the meantime, Dix continued his exploits. First, he captured a high ranking VC civilian official plus nineteen other prisoners. Next he led a rescue mission to the house of the Deputy Province Chief, quickly subduing the VC troops inside and rescuing the officials' wife and children.

Neither success in battle nor one's bravery can be quantified. Nevertheless, numbers do tell part of the story. Dix's actions led to as many as 39 VC soldiers killed, the capture of 20 prisoners, 15 weapons seized and the rescue of 14 civilians.

For his heroic actions on January 31st and February 1st, 1968, he received the highest accolade a member of the U.S. Military can receive, the Medal of Honor. He was the first enlisted man in Special Forces to have been accorded that high honor.

Following his extraordinary gallantry and highly effective leadership in Chau Doc Province, Dix received a direct commission as a first lieutenant. After a 20 year career in the army he retired at the rank of major.

Following retirement, Dix put his talents and experience as a counter-terrorism specialist to good use. While earning his living from owning and operating an air service in the Alaska interior, he continued to work in support of government-sponsored anti-terrorism programs.[xvi]

Following the attacks on America on September 11, 2001, security specialists, particularly those with a counter-terrorist pedigree, were at a premium. Dix found his talents to be in great demand. The federal government, individual state governments and private industry yearned for Dix's brand of expertise and moxey. Once you got past the usual patronage appointments of unqualified campaign contributors, cronies, relatives, friends, politicos, etc., who received appointments as homeland security officials, there remained a dire need for men of Dix's caliber. Thus, Drew Dix received the highly appropriate and well-deserved appointment as Commissioner for Homeland Security of the State of Alaska. In September, 2002, he was also chosen to head the state's Task Force on Homeland Security.[xvii]

The circle was complete. Almost 35 years after his exceptional contribution to the American cause in a war for which the public showed little enthusiasm, and at a time when Dix's exploits had long since faded from memory, his country was calling him again, this time to serve in the U.S. War on Terrorism, a cause his fellow countrymen almost universally embraced.

Eugene R. Ashley

Individual acts of courage throughout Vietnam during the Tet offensive are the stuff of legend. Most of them probably were never officially reported, or if they were, only to the command of the individual fighting unit. The suddenness of the attack forced the allied defenders in many cases into immediate action, without time to ruminate over what to do.

Imminent extinction sometimes summoned up a quality deep within the individual soldier, of which perhaps even he was not aware. Even afterwards, the heroic soldier at most times viewed what he had done as simply doing his duty. The real heroes were always individuals other than himself.

Such a man was Army Sergeant 1st Class Eugene R. Ashley, assigned to the 5th Special Forces Group (Airborne) , 1st Special Forces near Lang Vei. Another son of the south, Ashley was born on October 12, 1931 in Wilmington, North Carolina.

Sergeant First Class Ashley, a Senior Special Forces Adviser of an assault force, quickly and with a sense of extreme urgency, assembled an assault team on February 6, 1968 in order to attempt a rescue of other Special Forces advisers, trapped by the NVA, including his own commanding officer.

The NVA mounted an assault upon a hilltop ARVN and U.S. Special Forces Camp, known as Camp Lang Vei, which was five miles southwest of Khe Sanh and, therefore, right in the path of the NVA divisions conducting the siege of Khe Sanh.

Sergeant Ashley first helped fend off the attack with high explosives and illumination mortar rounds. Communications between the satellite and main camps were knocked out by NVA artillery. After first calling in air and artillery strikes on the invading forces, he realized that this would not be enough. A quick and cool thinker, Ashley received the inspiration to draw on the pool of local friendlies he had carefully cultivated as a military adviser. The reservoir of good will he had mustered enabled him to quickly organize a small assault team.

Ashley then led five powerful assaults against the NVA attackers, placing himself in harm's way each time, as the enemy forces directed dense and deadly artillery rounds, small arms fire and hand grenades into Ashley's small but intrepid group. The NVA left behind in their abandoned bunkers booby trapped satchel charges, which seriously impeded Ashley's progress, creating yet another way in which he and his men could die.

During his fifth and final assault, Ashley was forced to call in air strikes practically on top of his own team. But, it worked; the NVA were forced to withdraw, re-establishing allied control of the hill's summit.

Despite being severely wounded by machine gun fire, Ashley forged on, indifferent to concerns of personal safety.

After the fifth assault, his comrades carried an unconscious Ashley away from the summit only to fall victim to a fatal artillery round which landed in their midst.

The channel of escape carved out by Ashley in the enemy strongholds saved the entrapped Green Berets and indigenous forces, but at the cost of his own life.

For his extreme valor with utter disregard for his own safety, Sergeant Ashley received the Medal of Honor, posthumously.[xviii]

Sergeant Ashley was a true professional and at age 36 had reached the level of maturity where he would not recklessly place his life in danger. He was married, had attained a status in the Army which caused others to view him with respect and, in general, had a lot to live for. He placed himself in grave peril, not for glory, but simply because he saw it as part of his job.

As an African-American, he was one of an ever-widening circle of recognized true heroes of the military, who happened to be of the Negro race, a fact that might have stood in the way of his receiving the Medal of Honor in previous wars. The Vietnam War demolished such shameful barriers for all times.

2. The Battle for Hué

A major target of the NVA and VC during the Tet offensive was the ancient walled city of Hué in the Northeastern part of South Vietnam on the South China Sea.

At 3:40 a.m. on January 31, 1968, NVA and VC forces attacked the city of one hundred thousand people in great strength -seven to ten battalions supported by rockets and mortars.

Fortuitously for the invaders but unfortunately for the defenders a heavy fog provided protective cover. The fog combined with the element of surprise; and the help of NVA and VC collaborators within the city, granted the infiltrators a quick take-over of Hué, including the ancient walled Citadel, except for the headquarters of the South's 1st Vietnamese Army Infantry Division, which the ARVN was able to defend and hold.[xix]

Simultaneously, the 4th NVA Regiment was mounting a fierce assault upon the MACV compound in southern Hué. Reminiscent of the Battle of the Bulge, U.S. Army personnel consisting of clerk typists, supply sergeants, motor pool mechanics, communications specialists, chaplain's assistants and cooks were forced to join with the infantry elements assigned to MACV headquarters in fending off the attack. Miraculously, they held until relieved by elements of the 1st Marine Division.

On the morning of February 1, 1968 the red and blue banner of the VC flew atop the Citadel, but the ARVN and MACV headquarters were unconquered and still in operation.

All entrances to Hué were blocked and U.S. and ARVN forces would literally have to break into the city if they were to liberate it.

This was precisely what the allied forces set about to do and in the first major confrontation of the rescue effort, the 1st Marine Regiment, partnered with ARVN airborne forces, met the 806th NVA Battalion in battle at a blocking position on Highway 1, South of the city of Hué [xx].

Again proving the thesis that the VC and NVA were no match for allied forces in direct conventional warfare, the U.S. forces smashed through the NVA blockade and proceeded towards the Citadel encountering intense enemy fire for the entire length of the highway into the city. Other Marine companies and a tank platoon soon fortified the 1st Marine Regiment. Naval and ground artillery also bombarded the entrenched NVA and VC positions within the Citadel.

The battle raged on for ten days, from February 13th to February 28th, 1968, with street fighting every bit as arduous and bloody as that between the allies and the Germans in the cities, towns and villages of France during World War II.

U.S. and South Vietnamese Marines and the ARVN 1st Division cut a broad swath as they attacked across the entire breadth of the Citadel .

Finally, on February 24, 1968, the NVA and VC began to retreat. At 0500 hours on February 24th, the South Vietnamese red and yellow flag was raised atop the Citadel, replacing the VC flag.xxi

On February 25, 1968, the enemy's last position was overrun and the allied recapture of Hué was complete.

The human toll of the Battle of Hué was one of the worst of the War - including, in addition to all those who died or were wounded in combat, 116,000 persons rendered homeless and almost 6000 among the civilian population systematically murdered during the Communist occupation; and then thrown into mass graves. Again, the U.S. and South Vietnam had scored an impressive military victory; but at what price to both nations' collective psyches? Still another 1968 allied victory in battle was viewed by many as a psychological defeat.

Frederick E. Ferguson

The heartbreaking events of the Battle of Hué created an early despondency, followed by the elation of victory as the tide turned in the allies' favor; and finally a renewed sorrow when the full savagery of the NVA and VC assault against the civilian population became widely known.

The battles for Hué saw acts of heroism, far too numerous to chronicle. However, the actions of U.S. Army Chief Warrant Officer Frederick Ferguson were particularly noteworthy.

As Hué fell before the NVA and VC onslaught of January 30th and January 31, 1968, as part of the overall Tet offensive, a U.S. Army helicopter went down over Hué during a barrage of enemy antiaircraft fire. The crewmen and passengers of the downed aircraft managed to find refuge in a small, isolated ARVN compound. Before abandoning their downed craft, the crew also managed to send an emergency transmission to the headquarters of 227th Aviation Battalion, 1st Air Cavalry Division. Texas-born Chief Warrant Officer Frederick Ferguson volunteered to attempt a rescue without hesitation.

CWO Ferguson, an experienced pilot, commanded a re-supply helicopter. He was no stranger to landing his craft under heavy enemy fire but the concentration of anti-aircraft fire from enemy-occupied Hué was probably the heaviest of any battle in the south during the entire war. As Ferguson steadied his craft in a low-level course along the Perfume River, at maximum speed, and towards the ARVN Compound, he might well have compared his situation in terms of the intensity of the ground fire to Jimmy Doolittle and his audacious group of bomber pilots as they flew low over Tokyo amidst similar anti-aircraft fire in 1942.

Ferguson knew, however, what he was letting himself in for because he had been warned by all nearby aircraft to stay clear of the targeted area because of heavy anti-aircraft fire.

But, Ferguson was a pro and he confidently and unwaveringly maintained his course through a barrage of short-range fire from both enemy ground positions and boats. He was forced to employ every bit of his superior flying skill, coolness under fire and courage, to complete his flight and his mission in one piece.

He brought his craft in for a safe landing in a small, confined area, kicking up a blinding dust cloud to make his landing all the more difficult, all the while under intense mortar and small-arms fire.

As the wounded who had taken refuge at the ARVN compound were loaded on the helicopter, the craft took repeated hits from mortar fragments, causing heavy damage, but not quite enough damage to keep the craft from once again getting off the ground.

Chief Ferguson was not about to be deterred from the completion of his mission by damage to his aircraft as long as it could still get off the ground. If it could still fly he was determined to return the craft and its human cargo to safety. Hence, he took off in a hail of mortar fire, in a crippled aircraft, which flew straight through the same deluge of ground fire it had faced on the first leg of the trip.

Ferguson got all his passengers safely back to a friendly base, saving the lives of five of his comrades. His extraordinary actions, truly merited the Medal of Honor bestowed upon him for what he bravely attempted and accomplished on January 31, 1968.

3. Khe Sanh: Trapped in the Jaws of Death

"This extraordinary war in which we are engaged falls heavily upon all classes of people but most heavily upon the soldiers."

Abraham Lincoln

Khe Sanh belongs in the company of the siege of Bastogne at the Battle of the Bulge and the battle at the Alamo as one of the fiercest and most brutal sieges of an American installation in the nation's history. For 77 harrowing days, 6,000 United States Marines, surrounded and under non-stop bombardment and attack from a full division of 20,000 North Vietnamese regulars, fought a desperate battle for survival.

The Marine base at Khe Sanh and adjacent airstrip was situated on a remote plateau in the Central Highlands of South Vietnam, not far from the DMZ*. Purple Mountains ringed the forlorn outpost which was situated on flat land, with few natural defenses.

*demilitarized zone

Compounding the problem was the fact that the surrounding hills and mountains provided excellent offensive and defensive strategic positions for the NVA, from which they could fire artillery barrages, rockets and mortars into the base. The formidable problems of defending Khe Sanh under such circumstances raised grave doubts among the U.S. Military high command in Saigon and the Pentagon as to whether Khe Sanh was worth the very high cost in lives and material required to defend it. The Commander in Chief of U.S. Forces in Vietnam, General William C. Westmoreland, believed, however, that Khe Sanh was critical to U.S. control of Route 9, one of the few major highways of Vietnam, which in turn was key to American plans to cut off the north to south flow of supplies from North Vietnam to South Vietnam through Laos and Cambodia, along the Ho Chi Minh Trail (estimated at 60 tons per day).

Westmoreland believed that if he could interdict the Ho Chi Minh Trail, the entire North Vietnamese and Viet Cong military effort would collapse. Of course, he proved to be wrong in his assumption, partly because the Ho Chi Minh Trail was a complex web of different jungle paths and not just one clearly defined trail.

Khe Sanh was one of the most remote U.S. outposts of Vietnam. In early January of 1968, with Khe Sahn facing a full-scale siege by the NVA, the question being asked within the U.S. high command, despite General Westmoreland's strong views, was whether the base should be held or quietly abandoned. Along with President Johnson, American military officials decided to try to hold the base. On the morning of January 21, 1968, in an action that foreshadowed the general Tet Offensive 10 days later, NVA forces began their attack and the siege of Khe Sanh was underway. It proved to be one of the most brutal single battles of the war. The fighting raged for 77 days during which NVA rocket, artillery and mortar attacks were unrelenting.

To help defend the base the Marines had established defensive positions on various hills surrounding it. Intermittent battles between attacking NVA troops and outnumbered Marines had been in progress for many weeks before the actual siege began. Under cover of darkness on the night of January 20, 1968 and after midnight on January 21, 1968 NVA forces in an all-out assault tried but failed to overrun hills 881 south and 861 just north of the base. This thrust against the Marines outer defenses was followed by a massive artillery bombardment of the base a few hours later at 5:30 a.m. In its early morning barrage, the NVA scored a direct hit on the base's main ammunition store. Ninety percent of the U.S. artillery and mortar rounds were lost and 18 men were killed instantly. Scores more were wounded.

The besieged marines were faced with daily peril. The NVA bombardment was a constant from which there was no relief. Day after day, the enemy probed the base perimeter with assaults of 200 men at a time, with as many as 20,000 NVA troops poised to storm the base at all times. The Marines fought back fiercely and gallantly with mortars and guns; but without a constant flow of new supplies, it was clear that they would eventually be overrun by the NVA battalions. But, as re-supply by air had saved Bastogne in 1944, it also prevented disaster at Khe Sanh. U.S. C-130 Hercules Transports supplied Khe Sanh with 160 tons of supplies a day, the minimum required to keep on fighting.

Conditions inside the base were desperate. Food supplies were scarce and each man was restricted to two C ration meals daily. In order to survive, the Marines had to burrow deep into the earth, as no spot at Khe Sanh was safe. So, they dug into the ground and took up residence in fortified bunkers as deep as 18 feet below the surface. They no longer had the luxury of separate latrines, and the area outside each bunker became their toilet. There was no running water and no soap. Day after day the men were besieged by filth, stench, rats, fear of sudden annihilation, disease and exhaustion.

Typical of the constant peril they faced was the incident in which an NVA rocket landed in front of the command bunker. As later described by Artillery Commander Bruce Geiger, five Marines inside the bunker died instantly in the explosion.

As the siege wore on, the NVA inched closer to the perimeter by building miles of trenches and bunkers, a formula which had proved successful against the French at Dien Bien Phu. Ultimately, however, it was American air power which saved the day. U.S. B52's carpet-bombed the enemy positions causing massive damage to their trenches and bunkers. At the same time elements of the Army First Air Cavalry conducted air assaults into the hills surrounding Khe Sanh, landing in substantial strength of numbers in Huey helicopters and immediately engaging the NVA in ground combat.

The B52 bombing combined with the 1ˢᵗ Air Cavalry air/ground assaults and the massive U.S. relief effort was called "Operation Pegasus". It proved to be highly effective and forced the NVA to retreat from the area and back across the DMZ. Because of massive U.S. airpower, which the French did not have in 1954, the famous NVA General Vo Nguyen Giap was ultimately denied the same stunning victory he had scored against the French at the siege of Dien Bien Phu. The siege lasted for 77 days before the NVA finally abandoned their efforts and pulled out. The Siege of Khe Sanh was over.

The Apparitions of Dennis Mannion

Marine Corporal Dennis Mannion had been a forward artillery observer on Hill 861, which together with Hills 881 south and 881 north were essential to the protection of the Khe Sanh Marine base. He arrived at the hills overlooking Khe Sanh on or about 19 December 1967.

From late 1967 until the siege ended in April, 1968, the Marine positions on these hills were under constant attack by the NVA, who enjoyed vast superiority of numbers. Mannion witnessed the death of comrades during the fighting and wondered when his turn would come. Particularly hazardous were the U.S. sweeps of the surrounding areas, as far as the Laotian border.[xxii]

After the siege ended, Mannion gazed back at the top of the hill and saw what he thought were visions of 20 or 30 of the slain Marines wearing flak jackets and standing together in the mist and fog. Believing that he was simply experiencing an optical illusion, Mannion closed his eyes repeatedly but each time he opened them, the ghostly figures were still there. Such a specter had many precedents in American military history, perhaps the most celebrated having occurred in 1944 during the Battle of the Bulge when there were several independent sightings of eleven ghostly apparitions of German soldiers passing through the U.S. defensive perimeter around Bastogne, bearing no weapons and disappearing as fast as they appeared, as the snow fell from the night skies South of that besieged Belgian city.

Mannion became a high school teacher after the war and did his best to reassimilate back into civilian society. He wanted to put the war and Khe Sanh, Hill 861 and Hill 881s.[xxiii] behind him. But, in July 2000 he returned to Khe Sanh and Hill 861. Perhaps he was seeking closure by ridding himself of the haunting memories, or simply wished to honor his fallen comrades once more. The re-visit was an emotionally intense experience. On July 11, 2000 he spent 5 hours by himself on top of Hill 861 with "the wind, the mist, the memories, the history and the ghosts".[xxiv]

A poignant documentary film was made of his trip back to Khe Sanh, a base having long since disappeared without a trace; and to Hill 861, purged by nature of all signs of war and death.[xxv]

"I don't fight the battles anymore, but I haven't forgotten them... unforgettable really,[xxvi] said Mannion. And, he will never forget the ghostly apparitions of his fallen comrades.

In June of 1968, General Westmoreland, who was satisfied that U.S. forces had established a strong enough presence in the northern portion of the Central Highlands, near the DMZ, ordered the base at Khe Sanh dismantled and abandoned. Today it is nothing more than a grassy field interspersed with bomb craters in the earth and the remnants of the abandoned air strip. Nevertheless, it remains a popular tourist site and thousands, including many Americans, visit it each year to stand among the ghosts and echoes, the only permanent residents.

4. With Hearts of Lions:

John C. Liverman

Representative of the type of Marine who fought in Vietnam was John C. Liverman, who was killed in battle on December 11, 1968. It was especially poignant that he was felled only as the year was drawing to a close, because 1968 had been simultaneously one of the most tumultuous, dramatic, triumphant and yet sorrowful years in the glorious history of the U.S. Marine Corp.

The collective tenacity and fortitude of the Marine forces in Vietnam had enabled them in 1968 to endure and survive a 77 day siege at Khe Sanh, massive surprise attacks, isolation from support infrastructure and supply lines and fierce conventional and guerrilla warfare well behind enemy lines. Their losses were heavy but their victories were ultimately decisive and absolutely essential to the continued viability of the U.S. military effort. Those victories ultimately stood in stark contrast to the final lack of overall U.S. success in Vietnam.

Johnny Liverman, as he was called, had a happy childhood with loving, supportive parents and brothers surrounding him as he grew up in the Maryland suburbs of Washington, D.C. His father, Troy Liverman, became a soldier at age 17 and fought in World War II against the Germans, sustaining serious wounds from exploding German mortar shells. As far as Troy Liverman was concerned, the sun rose and set on his three sons. In fact, the Liverman family budget underwent serious strain so that the boys could be sent to parochial schools. The Liverman sons were graced with physical skills enabling them to excel in sports. They were living the American dream, with strong family ties undergirding solid individual accomplishments. No thought was given to the possibility that the dream would end prematurely, but then came the Vietnam War.

All three Liverman sons followed their father's example by volunteering for military service. Robert Liverman, now a corporate executive, volunteered for the Army and ultimately saw combat in Vietnam as a lieutenant. He was wounded after calling artillery fire onto his own position to suppress an enemy attack.[xxvii] James Liverman, like his brother John, also served in the Marines. Together the four Liverman men garnered three Bronze Stars and six Purple Hearts.

Johnny Liverman had it the toughest of all of them and the irony is that he could have avoided military service altogether as a result of having lost the cartilage in both knees from high school football injuries. But, instead of seeking to be excused from the draft, he volunteered for the Marine Corps as the war was heating up. Corporal Liverman reported for combat duty in Vietnam in January of 1968, just in time for the Tet offensive. His assignment was to the 1st Battalion, 9th Marines, the legendary "Walking Dead". Because his arrival in country coincided with the heaviest fighting of the war, Johnny was immediately sent into combat without preliminaries. By the end of April he had been wounded three times - a shrapnel wound to the shoulder, a second shrapnel wound and a serious gunshot wound to his thigh. The gunshot wound was the worst of the three and Liverman almost bled to death. The fighting was so intense that he could not be medevacuated from the combat zone for two days.

Johnny Liverman was sent to Okinawa to recover from his wounds. They were so severe that he could have stayed in Okinawa for the rest of his tour. It was not in Liverman's nature, however, to take the easy path, and after learning that a friend from his old unit had been killed in action, he volunteered to return to combat. It is one thing to demonstrate valor in the heat of battle, but without in any way diminishing any type of heroism, it takes a special type of hero to insist on returning to combat after just having won three Purple Hearts and having brushed with death in the process. In a letter to his father he offered the following explanation, "A job worth doing is a job worth doing right. I'm getting straight with myself. I have to go back and finish the job."[xxviii]

Corporal Liverman had to be acutely aware of the risks. He knew how fierce the fighting was and of the Marines' part in it. Two of his good friends and many other fellow soldiers had died in combat already and he had barely cheated death himself. But, back he went regardless, to the 2'" Battalion, 4th Marines in the dangerous region just south of the DMZ, where the NVA attacks were a daily occurrence.

On December 11, 1968 as Johnny Liverman's company engaged in a fierce and prolonged battle along the infamous Foxtrot Ridge, he took a bullet in the head. John Liverman never even made it out of his teens, but his age was a mere technicality. He was as much a man as anyone who had ever defended his country. He put himself in harm's way when a lesser man would have, with justification, taken himself out of combat. It is not clear where such men come from but in our current era of heroes with clay feet, who are often the inventions of the media and the entertainment industry, we all need to pay special thanks and feel humble gratitude, for the rare nobility of the Johnny Livermans of the world, without which our world and our lives might have been something very different.

Roy P. Benavidez

The memory of the warm, soft breezes gently blowing across the hills of South Texas, without disturbing the pristine quiet which enveloped the creatures in its midst, stayed with Roy Benavidez even during the fiercest combat in which he found himself in Vietnam.

As a former migrant farm worker, half Yaqui Indian and half Mexican, Benavidez saw himself simply as an American, anchored in the land and the nation which opened to him the road out of poverty and discrimination.

Due to ethnic prejudice, the marriage of Roy Benavidez's mother, a Yaqui Indian, to his father, a Mexican, was embraced by neither his mother's nor his father's family. Thus, from earliest childhood, Roy knew the sting of rejection from those who would normally have nurtured him with their love and attention.

The Yaqui were a tough, mean and ornery tribe. Even the cruel and fierce Cortes steered clear of the northern Mexican deserts to which the Yaqui were indigenous, during his conquest of Mexico in the 16th century. Cortes had no interest in engaging the Yaqui in battle. For hundreds of years the Aztec and Toltec tribes had been trying to conquer the Yaqui without success. The Yaqui had killed and eaten entire tribes of Aztecs. Ethnic Mexicans in Texas loathed the Yaqui and Roy's father's marriage was met with universal opprobrium from his family and friends.

Of course, even without intra-family hostility, Roy already had two strikes against him among the Texan Anglos, simply because he was Mexican. Their mistrust and bigotry had deep historical roots. In 1836, during the Texas War for Independence, a Texas general issued an order for the detention and exile of all Mexicans suspected of sympathy with the cause of Mexico. Nevertheless, Roy's great grand uncle rose to the rank of Captain in the Army of Texas under the command of General Stephen F. Austin.

By vocation, the Benavidezes were "Vaqueros", cowboys who had roamed the plains for 200 years before the gringos arrived in Texas.

Roy Benavidez was born in Cuero, Texas on August 5, 1935 into a family whose only sources of light in its unpainted frame house were candles and lanterns. His parents lived out on the plains far from even the smallest town, in complete isolation from the outside world. For food they raised chickens, kept a cow for milk and churned butter. They also had a small vegetable garden near their house.

A pivotal event in Roy's life occurred when his father died at a young age. This forced the family out of its self-imposed isolation as Roy's mother was forced to find work as a domestic to support herself and her two children. Roy also was forced to make his way in the world in his early teens. He dropped out of middle school and embarked upon a series of laborer's jobs that helped make him strong of mind, body and spirit. He loved the wild and beautiful rolling hills of south Texas and his cheerfulness of spirit helped him make friends easily. His parents had raised him to believe that all men were brothers and it became his conviction that distinctions of color, ethnic background, material wealth, geography and nationality, were meaningless. Said Roy, "When people probably hear my name, Roy P. Benavidez and think I'm a Mexican, or a Mexican-American, or a Hispanic, or a Chicano, or a dozen more names that I rather not mention, I call myself an American. [xxix] This powerful credo was central to Roy's character and he carried it with him when, as a young man, he enlisted in the United States Army.

Roy P. Benavidez served with the Army's elite in Vietnam -the U.S. Special Forces or "Green Berets". By May of 1968 he had risen to the rank of Staff Sergeant, assigned to Detachment B-56, 5th Special Forces Group (Airborne), Republic of Vietnam.

Consistent with Roy's belief in a brotherhood of men, he counted as one of his closest brothers, fellow Green Beret, LeRoy Wright, a schoolmate in the U.S. and a comrade in arms in Vietnam. Roy would later save his life in combat.

On May 2, 1968, shortly after the end of the Siege at Khe Sanh, a Special Forces reconnaissance team touched down safely by helicopter in a dense area west of Loc Ninh, along the Cambodian border. The group was known as a SOG team (Special Operations Group) and was composed of two American team leaders backed up by approximately 12 to 15 indigenous personnel. The team's mission was to gather intelligence information about a confirmed report that a large NVA force was active in the area along the border, which was controlled and routinely patrolled by the NVA. Not long after landing, the SOG team made direct contact with a battalion - size element of the NVA, made up of several hundred combat troops. A firefight broke out and the Special Forces team, vastly outnumbered, did the best they could to establish a perimeter and defend their position. Immediately they were pinned down by enemy fire and unable to move. They radioed for emergency extraction but the three U.S. helicopters which attempted extraction found it impossible to land in the face of an intense barrage of NVA anti-aircraft and small arms fire. They may, however, have bought the recon team time by drawing off some of the enemy fire to themselves.

Sergeant Benavidez was at a forward operating base in Loc Ninh when he picked up one of the radio calls from the team reporting their dire situation. When the helicopters returned to the base to unload wounded crew members, Benavidez voluntarily boarded a returning helicopter to take part in another rescue attempt. As they approached the LZ, he was acutely aware that the SOG team was likely crippled by casualties and unable to move to the pick-up zone. He urgently directed the aircraft to a nearby clearing where he jumped from the hovering helicopter. Armed with only a Bowie knife and bag of medical supplies, he dashed for about 100 yards under heavy small-arms fire to the besieged team. During his mad dash Benavidez was wounded in his right leg, face and head.

The hurting and hobbled Sergeant Benavidez was met by a scene of pure chaos when he arrived at the recon team's position. The team leader was dead and no one seemed to be in charge. Despite his injuries, Benavidez charged into the breach, assumed command, respositioned the team members and ordered them to redirect their fire so as to lay down suppressing fire on the NVA forces who were preventing the choppers from landing. This tactic proved effective and the extraction air craft were able to land. He then organized the loading of the wounded and dead team members onto the helicopter after having first thrown smoke canisters to direct the aircraft to the team's position. As soon as the helicopter touched down, Benavidez, ignoring his own wounds, carried and dragged half of the wounded team members to the aircraft. The pilot then moved to reposition the aircraft to get closer to the team's position in order to pick up the remaining team members. As they conducted this exercise, Benavidez ran along side the aircraft, all the while providing protective fire to facilitate the rescue of the remaining troops. He also managed to retrieve classified documents from the body of the dead team leader; but as he carried out this task, Benavidez was hit again by NVA fire directed at the team leader's dead body. He felt a hot and blinding flash of pain as enemy rounds pierced the flesh of his abdomen and back.

Then things went from bad to worse. At almost the precise moment Benavidez was hit, the pilot was mortally wounded and the copter crashed. Though critically wounded, Benavidez managed to make his way back to the wrecked plane. Sensing that they could move in for the kill, the NVA forces increased the intensity of their automatic weapons fire. The Special Forces team's perimeter was now at and around the wrecked plane. Sergeant Benavidez continually moved around the perimeter giving water and ammo to the men. It was only a matter of time, however, before the team's position would be overrun. Realizing this, Benavidez summoned up all the strength and will power he could muster and began calling in tactical air strikes from supporting gunships at the advancing NVA troops. The suppressing fire from the air was intended to reduce the enemy's fire power enough so as to permit another extraction attempt.

Just as another extraction aircraft landed, Sergeant Benavidez was wounded again, this time in the thigh, as he administered first aid to a team member.

Some NVA troops got close enough to the U.S. rescue scene to engage in hand to hand combat and Benavidez was clubbed by an NVA soldier on his head and arms before killing his assailant. By all rights that should have been the end of his fighting as he was carried, wounded and under fire, to the helicopter; but it wasn't. Upon reaching the aircraft he spotted and killed two enemy soldiers. Then, despite his many disabling wounds, Benavidez went back to the team's original position to make sure he had gotten all of the classified documents and rescued all of the wounded.

Finally, nearly faint-from loss of blood, Roy Benavidez let himself be hauled onto the extraction aircraft and returned to base. He had saved the lives of at least eight men. Back at the base, medics pulled over 30 metal fragments out of his body and patched up 100 some odd holes. He lay close to death and was not expected to survive but somehow the tough Yaqui-Tex-Mex pulled through; and in 1981, then-Master Sergeant Roy P. Benavidez, became the last American soldier to be awarded the Medal of Honor for gallantry in the Vietnam theater of operations.[xxx]

Roy P. Benavidez succumbed to a heart attack and passed away in 1988. His many grievous wounds sustained at Loc Ninh undoubtedly had a permanent debilitating effect on his overall physical health. His extraordinary valor in Vietnam, however, could not be easily forgotten. First, a United States Navy ship was named after him. Then, in November, 2002, the Valor Remembered Foundation teamed with sculptor, Mark Austin Byrd, for the creation of the Roy P. Benavidez Memorial Sculpture Project. Perhaps it is fitting that a man of stone be memorialized in granite for posterity.

Jacob (Jack) H. Jacobs

The young men who bore America's burden in Vietnam, like in all wars, were a cross section of "us". They didn't come mainly from one geographical region; they were not predominantly from a single race, religion, nationality, or ethnic group. After being sworn in to the U.S. military, they gathered in the train stations, airports and bus terminals of the deep south, the industrial heartland, the prairie states, the Pacific Coast, the frantic-paced northeast and everywhere else in America, in essentially homogenous groups of khaki or denim-clad men in their early 20's and late teens. Most carried a small bag containing only a change of socks and underwear, a toothbrush and shaving gear. They milled around, alone or in small groups, waiting to be transported to distant places like Fort Jackson, South Carolina; Fort Gordon, Georgia; Fort Dix, New Jersey; Fort Hood, Texas; Fort Riley, Kansas, Paris Island, South Carolina; or to naval bases in Charleston, South Carolina; Norfolk, Virginia and New London, Connecticut; and to Air Force bases in places like Champaign, Illinois, Pensacola, Florida, Plattsburg, New York and San Diego, California.

Among those gathered were farm boys, sons of the Appalachians and inner city kids, many of whom were barely-literate, mixing with young men of affluence as well as with the sons of the *vast* blue collar/white collar middle class.

Whether *any* particular one of them would become a good soldier had nothing to do with their backgrounds or circumstances, but rather flowed from some indefinable quality within the man himself, which could not be quantified, charted, graphed or reduced to a statistic. It was only in the experience of soldiering that the intangible would rise to the surface and separate some men from their peers, elevating them to an elite status.

The assembled men wore facial expressions, variously evidencing apprehension, excitement, nonchalance, nervousness, cockiness, loneliness, sadness, self-confidence and impassivity.

The expressions revealing some inner turmoil or upset were almost always genuine; those affecting toughness and cock-suredness were frequently just masks.

At some location in Trenton, New Jersey, in the latter half of 1966, waiting to be shipped out, was one of those young men, Brooklyn-born

Jack Jacobs, 21 years old and a newly-minted 2nd Lieutenant from the R.O.T.C. program of Rutgers University.

Jacobs was a studious young man, equipped with a high IQ and demonstrated academic talents. He could have been almost anything, and certainly law school, medical school and an MBA program at one of the nation's fine business schools were all within his reach.

But, in 1966 what America really needed was soldiers, especially those with the courage and capability to lead men in combat. So the Brooklyn-born, New Jersey-raised young scholar, Jack Jacobs, went off to war instead of to a university where he could burnish his intellectual skills and prepare for a lucrative and fulfilling civilian career.

It was in Kien Phong Province, Republic of Vietnam, that Jacobs's actions in combat rose to a level beyond the call of duty, at grave risk to his own life.

While a 1st Lieutenant with 2nd Battalion 16th Infantry, U.S. Army, Jacobs held the position of Assistant Battalion Adviser.

On March 9, 1968, only six weeks after the beginning of the Tet offensive, 2nd Battalion advanced on the Viet Cong as part of General Westmoreland's all-out Winter-Spring offensive.

Suddenly, the battalion came under intense machine gun and mortar fire as it moved toward the enemy. The thick and deadly fire was coming from a VC battalion safely ensconced in well-fortified bunkers.

With exploding mortar shells all around them and machine gun fire blistering their ranks, causing mounting casualties, the Americans became disorganized. Unless quick action by their leaders was taken, 2nd Battalion would be routed by the enemy.

Lieutenant Jacobs was in the thick of the action since he was with the command element of the lead company. First, his company commander went down from his wounds; and within a short time all of his senior officers were either dead or seriously wounded. Jack Jacobs was about to find out a lot about himself - to learn that he had that indefinable something which separated those who remained cool and decisive under fire from those who lost their composure. He quickly assumed command of the lead company and called in air strikes against the VC positions. This bought precious time for the allied forces to regroup and renew the attack. He also withdrew his unit to safety from the lethal combination of machine gun fire and mortar explosions.

But, Jacobs too had sustained a head wound from a mortar fragment. He was bleeding profusely from the wound and a steady stream of blood ran down into his eyes, clouding his vision. As Jacobs struggled desperately to maintain his vision through a cloud of blood, he caught a glimpse of one of his wounded men out in the open. Disregarding his own wound and impaired vision, Jacobs dashed toward the wounded soldier, all the while under intense VC fire. He reached the man, administered first aid and pulled him to safety. Jacob's courageous action saved the man's life.

Then quickly Lieutenant Jacobs went out again into the open to bring in several other wounded men, including his own company commander.

On three separate occasions Jacobs led his men to drive off enemy patrols looking for allied weapons and their own wounded.

In toto, Jack Jacobs saved the lives of one U.S. adviser and thirteen allied soldiers. Largely because of his actions, the lead company was restored to an effective fighting unit.

For his quick thinking and decisive actions under conditions of extreme danger to himself and his men, Lieutenant Jacobs received the Medal of Honor in 1969.

For his service in Vietnam he also collected two Silver Stars, three Bronze Stars and two Purple Hearts.

After his extraordinary tour of duty in Vietnam, Jacobs decided to stay in the Army, eventually retiring at the rank of Colonel.

Jack Jacobs had as successful a civilian career as a military career. Settling down in New Jersey, he married and had two sons and a daughter. He soon founded an auto finance company and became active in investment banking. His academic promise had already come to fruition before his retirement from the Army, when Jacobs served on the faculty of the U.S. Military Academy at West Point and the faculty of the National War College in Washington, D.C.

After retirement, Jacobs's civilian career in finance skyrocketed, landing him in the position of Managing Director of Bankers Trust Company.

Jacobs had assumed command and led his men to safety and then resurgence at Kien Phong in 1968. Those same leadership qualities enabled him to lead Bankers Trust Company's global investment program many years later to 2.2 billion dollars in assets. He also co-founded a similar business for Lehman Brothers, which enjoyed great success.

Today, Jack Jacobs has achieved a degree of celebrity in addition to his many solid accomplishments in business and public service. He is both a member of the Council on Foreign Relations and a military analyst for NBC/MSNBC.

Jack Jacobs is the prototypical citizen-soldier of the Vietnam era. He distinguished himself in battle and went on to also achieve great success in civilian life, among the best and brightest of his generation.

5. The Battle of A Shau Valley

The NVA attacks on Quang Tri and Hué during Tet led to a peripheral, yet none the less fierce, confrontation with the U.S. 1st Air Cavalry. NVA Forces exiting Quang Tri after the Northern city was re-taken by allied forces were interdicted by elements of the 1st Air Cavalry, resulting in many NVA regulars killed and captured in the A Shau Valley, Southwest of Quang Tri City.

Directly south of Quang Tri, the successful allied counterattack upon the walled Citadel of Hué caused a mass exodus of NVA and VC troops west into the A Shau Valley where the 1st Air Cavalry staged a blocking exercise to prevent their escape. These exercises turned into one of the biggest and bloodiest confrontations of the Vietnam War, known as the Battle of A Shau Valley.

Douglas B. Fournet

A native of Lake Charles, Louisiana, in the heart of Cajun country, Douglas Fournet entered the U.S. Army at New Orleans. On May 4, 1968, he had risen to the rank of First Lieutenant and was assigned to Company B, 1st Battalion, 7th Cavalry, 1st Cavalry Division, the proud airmobile fighting force that two and a half years earlier had so distinguished itself during the Battle of Ia Drang Valley. The "air cav" was now the stuff of legends with its distinctive patch and its cries of "Gary Owen". For Doug Fournet, it was a source of deep pride that he was not only a son of the South but also an officer in one of the finest infantry divisions in the world.

On May 4, 1968, Fournet, twenty four years old, was the rifle platoon leader of Second Platoon, Company B. In the uneven terrain of the A Shau Valley, taking and securing the high ground was often the key to survival. The battles there were not VC-style guerrilla warfare. Rather, they featured heavily armed and highly skilled infantry units pitted against each other.

Thus it was that Lieutenant Fournet and his platoon found themselves advancing uphill against a fortified NVA position. At intervals, 2nd Platoon was pinned down by enemy sniper fire and the going was slow and treacherous.

Suddenly, an alert trooper on the right flank of the advancing platoon spotted a claymore mine up ahead and directly in their path. The trooper instantly shouted a warning to his comrades. Realizing at once that the shouted warning would also alert the enemy, 1st Lieutenant Fournet ordered his men to take cover. He did not, however, take cover himself but rather ran uphill alone in the direction of the mine, drawing his sheath knife as he ran. His only concern was that his men were in grave danger. Shedding all considerations of personal safety, Fournet strategically placed his body in such a position as to shield his men in the event the mine were to explode. He then tried to disarm the mine by slashing the control wires leading from the enemy positions to the mine. Suddenly the mine exploded killing Lieutenant Fournet instantly. The five men of his platoon closest to the mine, however, were wounded only slightly when the mine went off. By sacrificing his own life, Doug Fournet saved theirs. For his bravery and self-sacrifice, 1st Lieutenant

Douglas B. Fournet became the first U.S. serviceman from southwest Louisiana to be awarded the Medal of Honor.

By act of the Legislature of the State of Louisiana in June of 2001, a 12.5 mile stretch of interstate 210 running through Lake Charles, Louisiana was renamed "The Doug Fournet Memorial Parkway".

Doug Fournet died far too young, 38 years ago. But, in the words of Longfellow, he left "a footstep in the sands of time" and the denizens of southwest Louisiana lobbied the State lawmakers into finally naming a highway after him, so that the flame of his memory might not flicker and be extinguished, but would instead attain immortality.

CHAPTER VII
A Strategy of Disengagement, 1969-1971

Richard M. Nixon was elected the 37th President of the United States in November of 1968, largely based upon his "plan" to win the Vietnam War and bring America's sons and daughters home. No sooner, however, had Nixon been inaugurated as President, than the NVA and VC launched a series of attacks in the South upon 125 targets, and bombardments of 400 objectives, in February of 1969.

As was the case during the Tet offensive a year earlier, the Viet Cong suffered a major military defeat at the hands of the Americans and South Vietnamese, but at a high cost to the U.S. - over 1000 Americans killed. Nixon retaliated by secretly bombing North Vietnamese encampments in Cambodia. The bombings, however, did not stay secret for long because the New York Times printed a report on the operations, further inflaming the anti-war movement, already greatly incited by the 1000 U.S. lives lost during the VC attacks.

In early 1969, the Nixon Administration had embarked upon a program it named "Vietnamization", designed as a gradual take-over of key military defenses and installations by the ARVN, who were to assume a steadily increasing share of the war effort, coupled with a phased withdrawal of American troops. The VC had been decimated by their massive losses during the Tet offensive and the February 1969 attacks and it seemed to be a propitious time to accelerate the transfer of the bulk of the fighting to the ARVN.

Events on the ground, however, prevented a smooth transition. In the face of Cambodian threats to evict the NVA from their camps and supply depots in Eastern Cambodia, the NVA, some 40,000 strong in Cambodia, sent an attack force toward Phnom Penh, the Cambodian capital.

Shock tremors from this provocative NVA action were immediately felt in Saigon and Washington. The professed reason for our presence in Vietnam was the "domino theory" - that the countries of Southeast Asia would topple like dominos in a row if Vietnam were to fall into communist hands. Now the very thing the U.S. had been fighting to prevent for eight plus years seemed suddenly to have become an imminent threat - the possible fall of Cambodia.

To ward off such a dire occurrence, President Nixon ordered U.S. troops to attack the NVA in Cambodia on April 28, 1970. On May 1, 1970 U.S. Forces moved against a network of NVA base camps and supply depots used to support NVA efforts in Vietnam. True to form, the target area was first covered with a carpet of B-52-delivered bombs. U.S. artillery also pounded the area. Then, as American armor advanced northward towards the objective, infantry units moved south and west against the same targeted strongholds and supply depots. If this weren't enough for the NVA to handle, the 1st Air Cavalry also dropped into their rear positions, completing the circle of chaos and destruction.

The Cambodian invasion was another smashing military success for the United States. Unfortunately, American military successes on the ground were dwarfed by consistent defeats in the court of American public opinion. Notwithstanding America's defeats and retreats on the psychological battlefield, however, the U.S. offensive into Cambodia was vitally important to overall allied strategy. The aggressive actions of the U.S. forces and ARVN prevented powerful NVA attacks from Cambodian sanctuaries into South Vietnam; and made it possible for President Nixon to keep his promise to withdraw one hundred and fifty thousand American troops from Vietnam.

The chain of residual benefits flowing from victory in Cambodia included the growth of Nixon's Vietnamization program, the postponement of an NVA attack upon South Vietnam for more than two years, the reduction of American casualties and the improvement in South Vietnamese morale.

Mitchell W. Stout

After the announced decision by President Lyndon B. Johnson in April 1968 not to seek re-election in the face of powerful opposition to America's involvement in the war among vocal segments of the population, command decisions were made to discontinue operations in various areas of South Vietnam. Khe Sanh was deactivated as a U.S. base approximately two weeks after the siege ended in April of 1968. But, General Westmoreland's objective of keeping Route 9 clear and viable was no less an imperative after Khe Sanh than it was before. Route 9 was vital to the support of operations in Northwestern I Corps. Khe Gio Bridge, located about 20 miles west of 1st Battalion, 44th Artillery Regiment headquarters at Dong Ha, was one of 49 bridges on Route 9. Its proximity to the DMZ made it vulnerable to attack and for that reason it was guarded by a contingent of 14 American artillerymen plus approximately 40 men of the 2/2 ARVN Regiment.

Intelligence officer Don Wittenberger was in the radio shack at Battalion headquarters at Dong Ha when the first ratio distress calls came through from Khe Gio Bridge on the night of March 12, 1970. It was clear that the U.S./ARVN perimeter had been totally breached by the NVA troops. In Wittenberger's words, "the frantic voice, heavy explosions and, stuttering gunfire mingled with radio static are forever etched in my memory."[xxxi]

The NVA's apparent plan was to penetrate the perimeter, pin the bridge's defenders down and freeze them in position with rocket and mortar fire and then annihilate them in their bunkers with grenades and other explosives. Part of the NVA's modus operandi was to permit the raining down of rocket and mortar fire on their own troops who had gotten inside the defenders' perimeter. The strength of the assaulting force was estimated to be 150 to 400 NVA troops.[xxxii] At the end of the day, the North Vietnamese attack was a failure from a purely tactical standpoint. They were not successful in either damaging the bridge or dislodging the U.S./ARVN garrison. It appears, however, that the real objective, not unlike the Tet offensive, was to accelerate the ongoing withdrawal by U.S. forces in Northern I Corps by inflicting as many casualties as possible. It may also have been a part of the North's overall strategy to "win the war in America's living rooms",[xxxiii] by demonstrating just how easily American positions could be overrun.

This macro-objective would certainly explain why the NVA was willing to accept such high losses at Khe Gio Bridge (approximately 40 known dead).

On March 12, 1970, Army Sergeant Mitchell Stout was only 5 weeks into his second tour in Vietnam. He was also only 16 days past his 20th birthday. Assigned to the 47ᵗʰ Infantry Regiment during his first combat tour, Stout was assigned in his second to 1st Battalion, 44th Artillery Regiment in the northern part of the Central Highlands. A native of Knoxville, Tennessee, he was solidly a part of the proud tradition of fighting men and women from below the Mason-Dixon line, who have in so many ways anchored the U.S. Armed Forces in the 20th and 21st centuries.

It was on a dark night at a lonely outpost *in* South Vietnam, when Sergeant Mitchell Stout, barely out of his teens, made the ultimate sacrifice for his country and his comrades.

As the NVA bridge assault was in progress, Sergeant Stout was in a bunker with four other members of a search light crew. The crew's position was first subjected to heavy mortar fire and ground attacks. The men then received what proved to be a false sense of relief as the mortar attack briefly subsided. However, as a seasoned combat pro on his second Vietnam tour of duty, Stout did not permit his senses, then on high alert, to relax in any way. With more combat experience than the other four soldiers in the bunker, Stout felt a personal responsibility for the safety of his comrades. He was their squad leader and they looked to him to teach them how to survive.

Suddenly, a grenade landed on the floor of the bunker. Stout reacted instantly and without hesitation. He ran to the grenade, picked it up and raced for the entrance. As he carried it outside, the grenade exploded at the same time that a mortar round landed nearby and exploded. Sergeant Stout was killed instantly.

In hindsight, even if the grenade had not exploded, Stout's chances of survival were slim. Post-incident interviews with survivors revealed that "the rain of shells was so heavy that no one could go outside without being killed instantly." Surely, the experienced and combat savvy Sergeant Stout was well aware of this fact.

Most remarkable about Stout's action was that he held the grenade close to his body, thereby shielding his fellow soldiers from the blast.

The results of Stout's extraordinary actions were tangible. In sacrificing himself he saved the lives of bunker-mates, Jimmy Silva, Robert Foster, Richard Dunn, and John Laughridge. All four men made it home from Vietnam alive and were able to lead productive lives because of the selflessness of Sergeant Mitchell W. Stout, U.S. Army.

Of the 14 Americans at Khe Gio Bridge, two were killed, five wounded and one captured. Sergeant Stout for his gallantry, was awarded the Medal of Honor.

Because he died in combat at the tender age of twenty years old, Mitchell Stout never had the chance to build an impressive biographical profile for himself. The information on the internet about him is scanty to say the least. For the sake of posterity, however, it is noteworthy that the U.S. Armed Forces did not forget what he did for his comrades and his country. His family and friends should be proud that in his memory the Brigade Headquarters building of the 4th Aviation Brigade, 1st Cavalry Division, Fort Hood Texas is named after Sergeant Mitchell W. Stout.

Joseph R. (Bob) Kerrey and
The Vietnam Syndrome

The exploits of Lt. Bob Kerrey and his seven man squad of Navy Seal Commandos were no more heroic than those of scores of other actions taken by brave soldiers, sailors, airmen and marines in Vietnam. The Bob Kerrey story, however, needs to be told if one is to even approach an understanding of the disabling paradox in which so many valiant Vietnam combat fighters found themselves. The unique Vietnam milieu had no historical precedent in America. In no other war since 1775 did such a large segment of the civilian population consider the conjoining of the words war and hero to be an oxymoron. The flawed logic went something like this: The Vietnam War was an immoral and unconstitutional war of wanton carnage instigated by arrogant and wrongheaded politicians in Washington and their corrupt puppets in Saigon. It follows that the only heroes were those who opposed the war and went to jail or Canada in protest. It, therefore, also followed that the American soldiers who fought in Vietnam, even those who distinguished themselves, cannot be classified as heroes because they were mere tools of a deadly and corrupt government policy. And, when their conduct on the field of battle resulted in the deaths of innocent civilians, especially women and children, the only thing for which they deserve commendation is their honest and open acknowledgement that atrocities took place in which they participated.

It does not take a genius to recognize what a slippery slope this type of specious reasoning creates. The descent down this slope has led to what has been called the "Vietnam Syndrome", a national affliction symptomized by an instinctive revulsion to U.S. military action in any part of the world and, in some cases, to all things military. The Vietnam Syndrome held America in its grasp through the late 60's, 70's and into the 80's.

Thus, when it was revealed 32 years later that Medal of Honor winner and United States Senator Bob Kerry, and his Navy Seal squad had opened fire upon and killed as many as 13 or 14 women and children on the night of February 25, 1969 during a commando operation in Thanh Phong in Vietnam's eastern Mekong Delta, calls were instantly made for an official Pentagon investigation of possible war crimes.

It is not surprising that no such investigation was seriously entertained. It is not the purpose of this book, however, to reach judgmental conclusions one way or another. The telling of the story of Bob Kerry in the Mekong Delta in 1969, like the telling of so many other Vietnam stories, is the only way I know to cut through the fog and mist of the Vietnam saga and its turbulent aftermath. Let the facts, to the extent that they can be accurately garnered thirty plus years later, tell the story.

On June 8, 1965, the United States Congress voted to permit the use of combat troops in Vietnam if South Vietnam requested it. By July there were 125,000 U.S. troops in-country. The military draft had been doubled by President Johnson to feed the insatiable hunger of the U.S. - South Vietnamese war effort for more and more troops. At about this time 21 year old Bob Kerrey was attending pharmacy school at the University of Nebraska at Lincoln but was contemplating changing his course of studies to religion. But, being a pharmacist or a theologian would have to wait as Kerrey pondered whether to enter the Navy's Officer Candidate School or simply wait to be drafted. Inspired by Herman Wouk's The Caine Mutiny, Kerrey chose the Navy with its promise of seafaring exploits.[xxxiv] Not unlike the decision-making process of other untold numbers of young men in wartime, a fateful, life-altering decision, had been made for an apparently casual reason - in this case inspiration received from a novel.

In October 1966, the asthmatic Bob Kerrey entered the United States Navy. In February of 1967 he said goodbye to his mother and father and to his native Nebraska and entered Officer Candidate School in Newport, Rhode Island. Shortly after being awarded his ensign bars in May of 1967, the motivated and idealistic young officer enrolled in the Navy Special Warfare Group, Pacific, for underwater demolition training. From there Kerrey was directly recruited into the Navy SEALS (acronym for sea, air and land), the Navy's equivalent of the Army's Special Forces.

Assigned to Navy SEAL Team One, Kerrey received six weeks of instruction in small arms and small unit tactics followed by Army Airborne and Ranger training at Fort Benning, Georgia.

Kerrey's long and intensive training coincided with momentous events in the war, both at home and in Vietnam. Antiwar protests in the U.S. occurred simultaneously with dramatic escalations in the number of U.S. service men and women in Vietnam, and with the number of casualties. A half a million American troops were on the ground when the NVA and Viet Cong launched the Tet offensive on January 30, 1968. Even before Tet American casualties numbered 1,000 a month. None of that phased the idealistic and gung ho Kerrey who longed to get into the action and put his training to use. Even as domestic support for the American effort waned during and after Tet and a demoralized President Johnson spurned re-election, Kerrey still itched to get into combat. Somewhat incongruously, the complex Kerrey was drawn to the Democratic anti-war presidential candidate, Eugene McCarthy, but decided that if Hubert H. Humphrey beat out McCarthy for the Democratic nomination, he would vote for the Republican, Richard M. Nixon, because of Nixon's alleged secret plan to end the war.[xxxv]

On January 5, 1969, his training finally completed, Bob Kerrey left for service in Vietnam. The highly motivated but enigmatic young Kerrey felt he was ready to go to war."[xxxvi] His destination was Cam Ranh Bay, the huge U.S. Naval Installation on the South China Sea. He became part of the Navy's Operation Market Time which was tasked with patrolling the entire coast of Vietnam, measuring 1,500 miles from the DMZ in the North to the CaMan Peninsula in the South.

Kerrey's dynamic commanding officer, Captain Roy Hoffman, was dissatisfied with the results achieved by Market Time and shifted the focus of the operation to the rivers and canals of the Mekong Delta, south of Saigon, under a new command named "Operation Sea Lord". The audacious Hoffman hoped to extend operations of his SEAL Team One" further up the Mekong River and deeper into the heartland.

Despite the general deterioration of U.S. troop morale, extensive drug use and racial tension throughout South Vietnam, none of this seemed to dilute the enthusiasm and high morale of SEAL Team One and Operation Sea Lord. The charismatic Captain Hoffman had his charges in a high state of readiness - "good to go", as the then popular expression went.

The paradoxically motivated yet ambivalent, Bob Kerrey, took his inspiration from the Civil War Union hero, Henry Abbott, of the Twentieth Regiment of Massachusetts Volunteers. Abbott did not believe in the Northern cause. He was, in fact, a member of the pro-slavery Northerners known as Copperheads. According to Abbott, and

Kerry too, soldiers must fight well and honorably even if they don't believe in the cause.[xxxvii] Hence, Abbott fought heroically for the North during the Battle of the Wilderness and was killed when he stood up to lead his men into battle.

Thus it was that a 1969 version of Henry Abbott, Navy Lt. Bob Kerrey, prepared his seven man Navy Seal squad to move by swift boat into the Mekong waters for an operation designed primarily to take prisoners for interrogation in an area of Thanh Phu province, reportedly controlled by the Viet Cong. Their mission would be carried out with no back-up from air or Naval gun fire. They were on their own.

The other team members were Mike Ambrose, the squad's usual point man; Gerhard Klann, the automatic weapons man; Lloyd Schrier, a medic; Rick Knepper; Gene Peterson and William Tucker.

Kerrey's squad had been unofficially dubbed "Kerry's Raiders" in recognition of the zeal of their young leader. Officially they were Delta Platoon, SEALS Team One, Fire Team Bravo.

On February 25, 1969, Kerrey and his team penetrated by swift boat deep into the lush and thick vegetation of the tropical Mekong Delta. Their objective was the Thanh Phu district, a free-fire zone reportedly infested with Viet Cong. Their mission was to kill or capture enemy soldiers or officials; their authority was to attack any targets of opportunity.

Both in 1969 and today, Navy Seals routinely conduct what are known as "takeouts", which are kidnap or assassination missions. On February 25, 1969, the "village secretary" of Thanh Phong was, according to military intelligence, to conduct a high-level meeting in Thanh Phong with a Viet Cong Military leader, the primary target of Kerrey's mission. Close to midnight on that dark night, Kerrey and his commandos silently took up their positions on the shore not far from Thanh Phong. After adjusting to the darkness Kerrey gave his team the order to move out. They were armed with M-16 rifles, side-arms, grenades, rocket launchers, a heavy-machine gun and knives. When they encountered a hooch that had not been mentioned in the intelligence reports, they used their knives to quietly kill the occupants who may or may not have been Viet Cong. Their standing operating procedure, however, was to either liquidate possible Viet Cong or Cong-supporters who might reveal their presence to the enemy, or to abort the mission.

Kerrey had no intention of aborting the mission. After neutralizing the hooch they crept along a dike for about 15 minutes towards Thanh Phong until they reached a group of 4 or 5 hooches. What happened next is not entirely clear in the fog of war but most team members have related that as they approached the hooches, many of the women and children inside emerged, began talking excitedly and Kerrey's squad began to take fire from the direction of the Hooches. Kerrey quickly gave the order for his men to return fire as they advanced on the hooches. [xxxviii] Under the rules of engagement imposed by Captain Hoffman, the squad could attack if they felt threatened. Kerry concluded quickly that the mission had been compromised. He was also convinced that "the armed cadre in the village were on full alert."[xxxix] (Kerrey, p. 184). On his orders, Kerrey's team "returned a tremendous barrage of fire and began to withdraw, continuing to fire."[xl] Kerrey witnessed women and children in front of him "being hit and cut to pieces", (Kerrey p. 184) screaming in agony.

Kerrey and his team retreated to the canal, alert to the possibility of ambush along the way. At the roughly appointed time and after Kerrey's signal, the swift boat picked up and returned the seven commandos to their base at Cat Lo.

The death of innocents was not unusual in guerrilla warfare and was a daily occurrence in Vietnam. None of that, however, was any consolation to the heart-sick Kerrey, who is haunted to this day by what happened on his watch at Thanh Phong on that moonless night of February 25, 1969. Approximately 14 women and children died violent, horrific deaths that night for having committed no greater sin than being in the wrong place at the wrong time. Bob Kerrey and his six other squad members all survived the war and assimilated back into peacetime America. Their trauma, wounds and death were more subtle than those suffered by the body. They were of things less tangible, such as the loss of their sense of a benign order in the universe, of the purity of their mission, of the integrity of their souls.

The incident was over but it wasn't. Each of the commandos carried the incident or some echo of it at varying depths of consciousness down through the years. Controversy flared in 2001 when team member Gerhard Klann related a version of what had happened thirty years earlier, greatly at odds with the official after-action reports. According to Klann, rather than returning fire as they approached the hooches, Kerrey's team, fearful that the women and children might alert the enemy soldiers if they let them go, rounded them up, opened fire and executed them, on Kerrey's orders, from a distance of six to ten feet.[li]

In a 2001 interview, team member Mike Ambrose repudiated Klann's version of the events. Ambrose stated that it was absolutely not true that the team had rounded up the villagers and slaughtered them. What he remembered was, "...we took a round somewhere near the back by Knepper and Peterson. Somebody yelled incoming. Once we received fire, we immediately fired."[xlii] The team was shooting from 20 to 50 feet away according to Ambrose. Only when they stopped shooting did he realize the dead were women and children.[xliii]

In April of 2001, the six other members of Kerrey's team denied Klann's allegations that they had executed the women and children. Their joint statement included the following:

"At the village we received fire and we returned fire. One of the men in our squad remembers that we rounded up women and children and shot them at point-blank range in order to cover our extraction. That simply is not true...We know that there was an enemy meeting in this village. We know this meeting had been secured by armed forces. We took fire from these forces and we returned fire. Knowing our presence had been compromised and that our lives were endangered we withdrew while continuing to fire."[xliv]

The historical context of the Thanh Phong incident is that the U.S. Military had assassination teams - operating under the Phoenix Program. Their target was usually the Viet Cong political infrastructure and the mission was to attack behind enemy lines and kill or capture Viet Cong officials and high-ranking officers. These missions were carried out mostly at night and the lines between combatant and non-combatant were often blurred in a war where old men, women and children might be equipped by the Viet Cong with weapons, employed as Viet Cong observers or used to set booby traps. Staggering as it may seem, some estimates had as many as 25,000 individuals assassinated as a result of Operation Phoenix.

The Navy SEAL commandos, like U.S. Army Special Forces, were elite units ordered to do the dirty work of the military - infiltration behind enemy lines, demolition, sabotage, capturing prisoners and assassination. Their missions were part of a ruthless phase of the Vietnam War and of all wars.

Acting in response to further intelligence on March 14, 1969, Kerrey led his team again on a SEAL mission to capture important members of the Viet Cong's political cadre. The objective was located on an island in the Bay of Nha Trang. To maintain the element of surprise, Kerrey and his team scaled a 350-foot sheer cliff to place themselves above the ledge on which they believed the Viet Cong were located. Kerrey then decided to split his team into two groups in order to garner the most effective force against the V.C. position. After giving instructions to both groups on how to coordinate their efforts, Kerrey led his men on a treacherous descent towards the VC encampment. As they neared the bottom of the descent, intense enemy fire was directed at them. Kerrey threw himself into firing position on the ground but as he did, a Viet Cong grenade exploded at his feet and threw him backward into the jagged rocks. Kerrey sustained massive injuries from the explosion which caused him to bleed profusely. However, wounded and against the rocks, he continued directing his team's fire into the heart of the V.C. camp. He also called in the second element of his team's fire support which caught the Viet Cong forces in a withering cross fire. After the enemy fire had been suppressed, he directed his men to secure and defend an extraction site, despite his being totally immobilized by his wounds and in a near unconscious state. Eventually Kerrey was evacuated by helicopter. His team had caused great havoc among the Viet Cong and they managed to capture enemy soldiers who later provided critical intelligence to the U.S. - ARVN cause. For his heroic actions on March 14, 1969, Navy Lt. J. Robert (Bob) Kerrey was awarded the Medal of Honor. Unfortunately, his foot was so badly mangled that it had to be amputated in the V.A. Hospital, thus ending Bob Kerrey's military career. He returned to his native Nebraska, recovered as best he could from his physical and psychic wounds, achieved great success in business, entered politics, was elected and served as Governor of Nebraska and eventually as United States Senator from the State of Nebraska. More recently he served as a member of the bi-partisan 9/11 Commission.

Kerrey's mission of February 25, 1969 had ended in tragedy and despair. His mission of March 14, 1969, a bare three weeks later, was a stunning success - a tale of adventure, daring and drama, which made

Bob Kerrey a national hero. The recognition and acclaim afforded to Bob Kerrey, could not, however, erase the shock, depression, guilt, emotional trauma and nightmares caused by the Tranh Phong bloodbath of February 25th. Such are the vagaries and contradictions of war. An entire generation of U.S. combat soldiers fought a ten-year undeclared war in a remote corner of the world. Fifty eight thousand of them did not come home. Of those who did return, untold numbers are still on an elusive search for inner peace.

Donald Farinacci

John E. Warren, Jr.

One of the enduring Hollywood stereotypes of World War II and Korean War movies was the kid from Brooklyn - the brash, tough-talking, frequently clownish character who always seemed to be right in the middle of every barracks and below-deck con or caper. He was always street-smart and tough, as loud and brash as he was loveable, but seldom a leader. He was far more likely to be played by a character actor like Cagney or Sinatra than a true leading man like Cooper, Gable or Wayne.

Of course, as much as the Hollywood version of the Kid from Brooklyn, with his unmistakable and totally unique New York accent, made for an entertaining character, he was hardly typical of most men from the city streets of America who have fought bravely in all of our wars. In fact, the gritty urban neighborhoods have produced as many outstanding leaders as any other geographical region of the country.

First Lieutenant John E. Warren Jr., a U.S. Army Infantryman, was a prime example of a kid from Brooklyn who distinguished himself by a selfless brand of leadership which had few equals.

John Warren was born in Brooklyn, N.Y. on November 16, 1946 at just about the same time as the U.S. military was in the process of being racially integrated, upon the order of President Harry S. Truman. Had John been born 20 years earlier and eventually served in the military during World War II, he would, as an African-American, been forced to serve in a segregated, all-Negro outfit. His chances of seeing meaningful combat would have been extremely slim, since the Pentagon generally viewed the Negro units as inferior. Of course, by 1946, the brilliant performance of all-Negro companies, battalions and regiments, such as the skilled and daring Tuskeegee Airmen, had demolished that biased perception forever.

Still, when 1st Lieutenant John E. Warren began his tour of duty in Vietnam on September 7, 1968, the racial integration of the Armed Services was only a little more than twenty years old and African-American officers were still far and few between.

Perhaps there was something almost mystical about the fact that Lt. Warren should have begun his tour of duty in 1968, that pivotal year in the Vietnam War and one of the most significant years in the history of our nation.

96

Relegated to second-class citizenship and, with some exceptions, subservience and obscurity, the Negro soldier, sailor or airman of W.W. II served and died beneath the radar, barely even noticed by the American public. Witness the brave African-American sailor, Dorrie Miller, who took over a gun turret and fired a SO caliber Browning anti-aircraft gun on the deck of the USS West Virginia, after all other able-bodied gunners had been killed or wounded; and in doing so shot down a Japanese plane during the attack on Pearl Harbor. His actual job was a menial one, below-deck as a mess attendant and ship's cook.

There was, therefore, a certain historical symmetry in the fact that in September of 1968, an African-American, 1st Lt. John E. Warren, Jr., was called upon to lead a fully integrated U.S. Army unit into combat during one of the most crucial phases of the most critical year of the Vietnam War.

1st Lt. Warren was a platoon leader of Company C, 2nd Battalion, 22nd Infantry, 25th Infantry Division, when he led his men into a fateful encounter with the enemy in Tay Ninh Province, Republic of Vietnam, on January 14, 1969.

In the final analysis a man's story is uniquely his own, having little to do with history, sociology, race, nationality or culture.

Whatever it took for 1st Lt. John E. Warren, Jr., while under ambush by well-fortified VC units protected inside their bunkers, to rally his platoon on January 14, 1969, and to maneuver and charge into the teeth of the enemy's fire, belonged exclusively to him, the product of his own special make-up as a man. What happened next demonstrated that a major ingredient of that make-up, of his singular character, was an extraordinary quality of selflessness and love for his men. As he came to within six feet of one of the VC bunkers, and was preparing to toss a hand grenade into it, an enemy grenade landed in the midst of Warren's platoon. The instinct for survival is strong in all men. But, a counter-instinctive act of self-sacrifice propelled Warren to lunge and fall in the direction of the hand grenade, thereby turning himself into a human shield and saving the lives of many of his men, at the inestimable cost of his own. John E. Warren, Jr. in a split second had become a man for the ages. His action performed in that fraction of a second was an eloquent statement of the kind of man he was.

Fortunately, America had grown up enough by 1968 to possess the maturity as a nation to proclaim his gallantry, unlike that of Dorrie Miller, the Pearl Harbor hero who received the Navy Cross but was denied the Medal of Honor, solely because of his race.

John E. Warren was awarded the Medal of Honor for his bravery and self-sacrifice, posthumously. His pure gift to his men, that of his own life, was as generous as any man has ever given, or will ever give. John E. Warren, Jr. was only 22 years old but in that frozen segment of time on January 14, 1969, he also left, in the words of Longfellow, "a footprint in the sands of time"; beside those left by the men of Bunker Hill and at Yorktown; at Antietam, Gettysburg and Chancellorsville; at Verdun and Belleau Wood; on Anzio Beach, Normandy, The Bulge and Iwo Jima; at Inchon and Chosen Reservoir; in the Ia Drang Valley, Khe Sanh and Hué and at thousands of other places.

After the life and death of John E. Warren, Jr. new footprints were added at places like Kuwait City, Tora Bora and Falluja - the imprints of a vast army silently marching down through time, our protectors, our heroes, all gathered together with the spirits of Dennis Mannion, floating above us in the mist.

Louis R. Rocco

Socrates opined that an unexamined life is not worth living. Maybe that's true, but whether Louis R. Rocco took the time for introspection or not, his life was truly well-lived by anyone's standards.

Oddly, however, it didn't start out that way. Born and raised in an impoverished region of southern New Mexico, Rocco's family was so mired in poverty during his youth that there seemed no way out.[xlv]

As a teen, Rocco, who preferred his middle name, Richard, drifted into trouble with the law and appeared headed for a life of petty crime when fate intervened. Rather than serving a jail term for his latest offense, the court allowed Richard to enlist in the Army after a kind-hearted recruiter intervened on his behalf. In 1956, at the age of eighteen, Richard Rocco entered the United States Army and after basic training, went on to be trained as a medic. He later had the opportunity to re-pay the same recruiter by treating him for his wounds in Vietnam.

By May of 1970 Richard had advanced to the rank of Warrant Officer and was serving a tour of duty in Vietnam when an urgent mission was being hastily organized to evacuate eight critically wounded ARVN soldiers. Without hesitation, Rocco volunteered to join the medical evacuation team. An Army helicopter carrying Rocco and the other members of the team was soon airborne and flying low over a VC--infested area northeast of Katum in the Republic of Vietnam.

As the helicopter approached the landing zone, "we started taking fire from all directions", Rocco recalled during an interview conducted by the American Forces Information Service in 1998.[xlvi] There was no aborting the mission, however, and the aircraft descended towards the LZ.

Rocco knew that if they had any chance of landing in one piece he better take matters into his own hands. He and other members of the team began a barrage of accurate suppressing fire upon the enemy positions.

Nevertheless, the helicopter had taken some major hits and was forced to crash land. Upon impact with the ground, Rocco felt a bolt of excruciating pain knife through his hip and wrist, both of which were broken by the force of the crash. He was not about to dwell on the pain for even a second, however, because he was both lucky to be alive and in grave danger of not staying that way for long.

"The pilot was shot through leg", recalled Rocco during the interview. "The helicopter spun around and crashed in an open field, turned on its side and started burning. The co-pilot's arm was ripped off - it was just hanging."[xlvii]

Four other crew members were also shot. Acting on reflex, Rocco pulled the pilot out of the plane and then jumped out himself. Looking for cover he sighted a felled tree lying on the ground. "I dragged him to the tree, knowing that at any time I was going to get shot."[xlviii]

After bringing the pilot to relative safety, Rocco returned to the aircraft and, under a continuous hail of fire, carried the copilot, the crew chief and a wounded medic to a position of cover, one man at a time.

Soon the flames of the burning helicopter, which had burned Rocco's hands and face as he struggled to remove his three unconscious comrades from the aircraft, engulfed the craft entirely. Had it not been for Rocco's heroics, the pilot, co-pilot, crew chief and injured medic would have all perished in the flames. As it turned out, Richard Rocco had carried each man to safety across approximately 20 meters to the ARVN perimeter, under intense enemy fire, while he himself had a broken hip, a broken wrist and burned hands. He simply ignored his own excruciating pain so that it would not interfere with saving the lives of his comrades.

Once he had accomplished that mission and all were safely within the confines of the ARVN perimeter, Rocco administered first aid to the wounded until his own wounds and burns caused him to collapse and lose consciousness.

The next day all five Americans were rescued from the besieged ARVN position but only after two American helicopters were shot down in an attempt to evacuate them. "They didn't have time for litters or anything else. They just threw us into the helicopter and took off," Rocco also recalled during his 1986 interview.[xlix]

While hospitalized for his burns and injuries during May and June of 1970, Rocco got wind of the fact that he had been recommended for the Medal of Honor. But, he dismissed it from his thoughts when he heard nothing more about it for several years. Little did he know that all the while the co-pilot he saved, Lt. Lee Caubarreaux, had been tenaciously lobbying in Rocco's behalf.[1]

It seems that the Medal of Honor recommendation which Caubarreaux had so strongly supported had been mislaid. Fortuitously, in March 1971, it was mailed to Caubarreaux by a warrant officer who found it in a desk drawer almost on the eve of Caubarreaux's medical retirement from the Army.

Mr. Caubarreaux would no more be deterred from pursuing the award recommendation than Rocco had been in pulling him to safety. He lobbied both the Army brass and Senator Russell Long of Louisiana, his home state.

Finally, Mr. Caubarreaux's efforts came to fruition, when President Gerald R. Ford bestowed the Medal of Honor upon Richard Rocco on December 12, 1974.

The military had truly become home for Richard Rocco and he made it his career. He retired in 1978, only after 22 years of service, with the rank of Chief Warrant officer.

True to Rocco's life-long commitment to the military and to his country he re-enlisted in 1991 during the Persian Gulf War.

After his final retirement Rocco was free to pursue his other great passion, veterans' affairs. By the time of his death in 2002 at the age of 63, Richard Rocco had become a legend of veterans' advocacy. He shrewdly parlayed his Medal of Honor into a host of successful programs to ease the pain of physically and emotionally impaired veterans.

In his home city of Albuquerque, Rocco started a Vet Center *on* Fourth Street. One of Rocco's best friends, Marine Corps Veteran Pete Stines, told the Albuquerque Tribune after Rocco's death, "I've known Richard since 1978 when he started the Vet Center on Fourth Street. I went there because I needed help. He understood where I was coming from with my problems of post-traumatic stress disorder. He was that way with everyone - trying to help them with their fears and anxieties."[li]

Rocco was tireless in his efforts on behalf of Veterans, starting a shelter for homeless veterans as well as a nursing home. As a lobbyist he successfully brought about tuition waivers for veterans attending state-run colleges.

As recognition for his skill and dedication as a veterans' advocate, referred to by some as an "angel on earth", he was named as Director of the New Mexico Veterans Service Commission.

In the years prior to his death from lung cancer, Richard Rocco was forced to scale back some of his more strenuous efforts on behalf of veterans due to his declining health. But, by then Rocco's legacy was firmly imprinted upon the public consciousness. "Richard was a hero while serving in Vietnam. He was even more of a hero to our veterans when he came home", proclaimed United States Representative Heather Wilson[l]" in recognition of his exemplary life.

Even as his health failed in his later years, Rocco worked in programs and activities designed to keep children away from drugs and violence. Community leaders were unanimous in their estimation of Richard Rocco as a perfect role model.

As a tribute to his long-time service to the community, a park next to the Albuquerque West Side Community Center was re-named The Richard Rocco Medal of Honor Park. Rocco referred to the ceremony in his own simple but heartfelt words as "an honor that I hold above presidents and legislators because these are my people. For them to honor me, it makes me feel so good."[liii] One of those people was Army veteran and long time friend, Al Valdez[liv], who proclaimed, "A medic's primary duty is to save and protect. Richard spent his whole life healing." Stines added that Richard Rocco "was the kind of person you looked up to as "a mentor, a friend, a buddy - someone who would do anything for you. And you knew that he would because he'd already done it.

Mr. Caubarreaux, the helicopter co-pilot who owed his life to Richard Rocco, was also fortunate to have his shattered arm saved by doctors. In 1998 he told The American Forces Information Service that if not for Rocco, "we would have burned to death in the helicopter. I can't screw in a light bulb with my arm but I can still hug my wife."[lvi]

Richard Rocco had a wonderful life - for himself and for those he touched.

CHAPTER VIII
Exodus 1970 - 1972

President Richard M. Nixon had campaigned on a pledge to end the Vietnam War and told the electorate that he had a "plan".

Nixon and his National Security Adviser, Henry A. Kissinger, wasted no time following the Inauguration in January of 1969 in working the problem. Nixon had seen how the war had totally exhausted and demoralized his predecessor, Lyndon B. Johnson, and did not wish to share the same fate.

Before taking specific measures, Kissinger and Nixon decided it was prudent to take a sampling of opinion throughout the military and the Washington governmental establishment. To this end, they sent a memorandum in the form of a questionnaire to the Pentagon and various government agencies, posing detailed questions about the war and how it had been conducted. However, before the new team even had a chance to evaluate the answers, Ho Chi Minh and General Giap preempted the process, as they had done so many times to Johnson, McNamara and Westmoreland, by launching a series of widespread surprise attacks throughout South Vietnam. The targets of the assaults included U.S. installations, with the two-fold purpose of disrupting the pacification program which had been making some progress and elevating the U.S. body counts.

Ho and Giap had shrewdly taken the pulse of the American public and knew that it was sick of the war - of American soldiers coming home in boxes, of the nightly grisly images of violence, death and dying flashing across their T.V. screens, of the fracturing of American society caused by widespread dissent over the war and of the sheer brutality embodied in incidents such as the Mai Lai Massacre and naked children running down a road, their clothing burned off by napalm.

The Vietnam War was the first one Americans actually got to visually witness each night on television and what they saw was deeply unsettling.

Nixon was furious over the early 1969 NVA attacks, which violated an informal agreement with North Vietnam. Any illusions he had harbored concerning an early end to the war and a quick exit from Southeast Asia had been smashed by the NVA offensive. It set the tone for everything that was to follow. Nixon knew that he had to end the war if his presidency was to be considered a success but by mid-February of 1969 he also knew that it wasn't going to be easy.

His mistrust of the North Vietnamese ran deep and his exit strategy, if indeed there ever was one, dissolved into a series of fits and starts which played themselves out over the better part of the next three years. They included as a precursor to the U.S. withdrawal of 150,000 troops from South Vietnam, the secret U.S. bombing of Cambodia and the U.S. ground and air offensive into Cambodia, preventive measures geared to discourage a massive attack by the NVA upon South Vietnam following the American troop withdrawal.

The troop withdrawal was just one part of President Nixon's policy of "Vietnamization," the phased-in, gradual turn-over of the conduct of the war and the pacification of the war-ravaged regions of the South, to the South Vietnamese military and civilian establishments. It took Nixon four years to turn the ARVN into an independent fighting force. Even so, once American air support was withdrawn in 1973, South Vietnam was defeated by the NVA.

The length of the war, the excesses of the anti-war movement and the perception of a no-win policy all combined to severely damage the morale of the troops. Add to that the nature of the fighting itself with American soldiers witnessing daily their comrades being killed by an unseen enemy suddenly firing from hidden positions behind thick foliage and then just as quickly melting away into the jungle. Even if the enemy was out in the open he couldn't be easily identified. Any man, woman or child could be VC. Any hutch or village well could be booby-trapped.

Any old man or young boy who stared at the passing troops on a search and destroy mission could have simply been conducting reconnaissance for VC or NVA troops up ahead, lying in ambush.

U.S. troop morale began to precipitously decline in 1969. Drug abuse by American soldiers became commonplace. By 1970, desertions and absences without leave were steadily on the incline. Many soldiers could simply not envision how the war, at the end of its second decade, could lead to any positive good.

Frustrated and demoralized by the unending cycle of death, destruction, weak support from the homeland, poor leadership and the inequities of the draft, which placed a disproportionately high number of African-American soldiers in infantry units, an unusually high number of soldiers, sailors and airmen lapsed into serious disciplinary problems. The prevalence of drug offenses and other forms of misbehavior led to a dramatic spike in court-martials and unit-level punishments.

By 1971, it was clear that the wheels were coming off the bus. Morale both in the United States and among the troops in Vietnam had reached an all-time low. One hundred and fifty thousand people staged a massive anti-war demonstration in San Francisco. Two hundred thousand protestors poured into Washington and set up camp on the south mall, within sight of the Lincoln Memorial. The Mansfield Amendment, sponsored by the popular senator from Montana, Mike Mansfield, was passed by the U.S. Senate and called for the removal of U.S. troops from Vietnam at "the earliest possible date."

Throughout 1971, Henry Kissinger and Le Duc Tho, North Vietnam's chief negotiator, engaged in so-called peace negotiations. The problem was the North Vietnamese didn't really want peace - they wanted victory.

As the negotiators dickered over trivial issues, the Soviet Union continued to supply North Vietnam with massive amounts of weapons, ordnance, planes, tanks, anti-aircraft missiles and other supplies.

By the end of 1971, an extremely well-armed and well-supplied NVA was poised along the 17th parallel, ready to launch a massive attack on the South. As soon as it was fully deployed, Le Duc Tho abruptly cut off negotiations with Kissinger. When the attack came Nixon immediately ordered the resumption of heavy bombing between the 17ᵗʰ and 18ᵗʰ parallels, hoping to slow down the twenty NVA divisions headed for the border.

So it went, into the Spring of 1972. U.S. forces in all of Vietnam had been reduced to no more than 130,000 men. The vastly superior NVA was in position in many strategic regions of the Northern part of South Vietnam to attack and destroy the remaining allied forces. They could not do so, however, because of superb U.S. tactical airpower which was capable of raining destruction upon them anytime and anywhere.

The massive NVA attacks across the 17ᵗʰ parallel in April 1972 led to the capture of Quang Tri city, only to have it recaptured by the ARVN with massive U.S. B52 bomber support in May. B52 bombing also stopped the NVA dead in its tracks when it attempted to overrun Kontum. U.S. airpower was proving to be the equalizer in creating stalemate between the competing forces of the North and South.

Le Duc Tho was forced to initiate peace talks with Kissinger, which continued from July through October of 1972. American bombing had forced Tho back to the negotiating table. A draft of a purported peace agreement was hammered out leading Kissinger to make the dubious declaration, "Peace is at hand". By mid- December, however, the draft agreement, which contained all kinds of hidden traps for the allied forces and escape hatches for the North Vietnamese, was no closer to a final draft acceptable to the U.S. and South Vietnam.

The U.S. then upped the ante by twelve days of B52 bombings which reduced much of North Vietnam's industries and military sites to rubble. They came to be known as the "Christmas Bombings". A month later Hanoi agreed to a cease fire and a "peace" agreement was signed on January 23, 1973, referred to bitterly by South Vietnamese President Thieu as a "surrender agreement". Thieu's characterization was pretty close to the mark since by its terms the United States was required to remove all of its armed forces from South Vietnam within sixty days while Hanoi was allowed to leave its forces in place in South Vietnam. Despite its many flaws, the Paris Peace Accords were formally signed on January 25, 1973 and the U.S. began its withdrawal from South Vietnam, in effect a U.S. retreat caused not by conditions on the battlefield but rather by conditions on its own home soil. A tragic chapter in American history was drawing to a close.

Harry W. Horton, Jr.

"Not for fame or reward, not for place or for rank, but in simple obedience to duty, as they understood it."
Confederate Memorial Arlington National Cemetery

The unceremonious disengagement of the United States from the Vietnam War in 1973 was just one more blemish on a national policy gone awry. But, as embarrassing as it was for the civilian and military architects of United States war policy in Vietnam, most of the troops on the ground had nothing to be embarrassed about. To the contrary, the overwhelming majority of them acquitted themselves admirably and honorably.

Unfortunately, just as it would be impossible to properly honor the heroes of all the wars in which the United States has fought, it is equally impossible to pay proper tribute to all of the valiant men and women who performed acts of selflessness in Vietnam in what they saw as the protection of their country and of each other. Many, if not most, of those acts of heroism never received wide acclaim and are known only to the participants and to some of those directly benefitted.

I believe, however, that the stories depicted in this book are representative of the brand of unselfishness and courage displayed by most of the heroes of the Vietnam era. It was the men and women of the U.S. military who did their duty, honorably and without fanfare, who comprised the overwhelming majority; not the perpetrators of war atrocities, habitual drug abusers and malingerers, drunken rowdies in the night clubs of downtown Saigon and those who displayed indifference in the face of the enemy.

It has become common in recent books, movies and television shows to state unequivocally that in the final analysis what men in combat fight and die for is each other and not for an abstraction such as patriotism. There is some truth to that but it is not the whole truth. Great acts of patriotism by U.S. military personnel have been common in all America's wars. Without patriotism our country would not have survived as a strong and free nation. This is not to say that there is only one brand of patriotism. Indeed, a powerful argument can be made that those who risk imprisonment by peaceably protesting an unjust war are just as patriotic as those who elect to fight in that war.

Patriotism can be an elusive concept but sometimes the facts of a particular individual's story are so compelling that the story serves as a metaphor for an entire group. Lieutenant Harry Horton's story was a metaphor for the best of the Vietnam era generation of young Americans.

Harry W. Horton, Jr. was not a charismatic leader, was not showy and was not a big talker. He would never stand out in a crowd. He simply believed in quietly doing his duty regardless of the personal risk involved.

"I'm dead", said Army 2nd Lieutenant Harry W. Horton, Jr. to his OCS roommate, B. G. Burkett, upon reading his orders for Vietnam. Burkett was hardly surprised by Horton's proclamation since throughout officer candidate training Horton had repeatedly stated his conviction that he would be killed in Vietnam.[lviii]

Perhaps concerned that his friend's certainty that he would die in Vietnam could become a self-fulfilling prophecy, Burkett asked him one night during training why "if he believed he was doomed to die in combat - he had not taken one of the ways out many others had taken, heading for the Canadian border or faking a medical condition." Horton's simple reply was "Because America needs me".[lix] Burkett had not the slightest doubt that Horton meant every word.

Horton, in effect, made an unwritten last will and testament the night before he left for Vietnam by dividing up his few possessions among his three OCS buddies, including Burkett.

About a month later, in December of 1967, Burkett sent Horton a Christmas card, but it came back marked "Deceased".[lx] Harry W. Horton, Jr., a Second Lieutenant with Delta Company, 3rd Battalion, 22nd Infantry Regiment, 25th Infantry Division died in combat with thirteen other members of the 3rd Battalion on December 22, 1967 as he led his rifle platoon into battle. He was 22 years old.

A native of LaMarque, Texas, Horton dropped out of the University of Texas in 1967, enlisted in the Army and attended OCS, after which he was commissioned a 2nd Lieutenant.

As Delta 3/22 moved forward to engage the VC on a search and destroy mission on December 22, 1967, his platoon was ambushed and forced into a defensive position from which it could not move without sustaining heavy casualties. 2nd Lieutenant Horton, in an effort to save his platoon, single-handedly charged an enemy machine gun bunker. He was mowed down by enemy fire and was killed.

Harry Horton was an everyman in most ways. He wasn't brilliant, athletic, handsome or particularly popular. But what set him apart from most was the sincerity and depth of his patriotism. It is one thing to be fearless in battle. It is quite another to be filled with fear yet refuse to give in to it. Such is the epitome of true personal courage.

Harry Horton, convinced he was a dead man walking, nevertheless, because America needed him, overcame those fears and dashed headlong into the teeth of enemy machine gun fire. He believed America needed him to do that to defend his country and protect the other men of his platoon; and that was what mattered to him.

Harry Horton exemplified the difference between bravery and bravado. Had he lived he would never have exploited the Silver Star he was later awarded, posthumously, to achieve fame or riches. Hollywood would never have type-cast him as the typical war hero. He was simply too ordinary and his deeds on the battlefield may have been little-noticed.

But that is exactly the point. It was not Harry Horton's words, appearance, manner or personality which defined him. It was his deeds - those of extraordinary personal courage of the type which have protected and saved this country through perhaps a dozen major wars during its 231 year existence. In a sense, Harry Horton's life and death on a larger scale was also a metaphor for the quiet dedication and courage of the legions of ordinary heroes who have served and died so that the rest of us might live in peace and comfort.

I had the rare privilege of serving with some of those ordinary heroes from August of 1966, to August of 1969. May we never forget them.

EPILOGUE
The Fall Of Saigon

In March and April of 1975 South Vietnamese Military Regions I and II fell before the onslaught of the attacking NVA. The ARVN 18th Division, then waged a valiant defense of Highway 4, southwest of Saigon against four NVA divisions and held out for thirteen days. They were finally forced to retreat but only after killing five thousand NVA soldiers.

On April 21, 1975, South Vietnamese President Thieu resigned and fled the country for Taiwan. The final surrender by South Vietnam followed soon afterwards.

On April 30th, Americans still in-country were evacuated by helicopter together with certain selected South Vietnamese officials, amidst bedlam and chaos, as Saigon fell to the NVA.

As part of the evacuation two hundred U.S. civilians and military personnel were air lifted from the roof of the U.S. Embassy and other parts of the grounds to the airfield at Tan Son Nhut. A communist flag was raised over Independence Palace. The war was over. South Vietnam had fallen to the Communists. Saigon was renamed Ho Chi Minh City, the name it still bears today.

For the United States, a long, arduous and searing chapter of its history was closed. No single postscript can sum up the fear, horror, anguish and grief suffered by United States military personnel who fought in Vietnam and their families.

But the reminiscence of Joseph G. DiBernardo of Stony Brook, New York, who served with the U.S. Army First Infantry Division in Vietnam from 1965 to 1966 provides as vivid an epitaph to the U.S. Vietnam saga as any:

"I remember the heat, the bugs, the snakes, spiders, scorpions... Rain and mud, ate c-rations all the time, no hot food, no showers...I remember the sheer terror of a firefight, the fear of mines and booby traps in the jungles and on the roads...how luck played a hand, a couple of inches either way and you get your head blown off, be one or two guys back in the column and the mortar hits you...How tight all the guys in your squad were...how some guys were brave and some were not...how some officers and non-coms were inept and some low grunt was a leader. Most of all I think how what a waste it all was...all those guys that did not come home and look at what is going on today with them. Let the generals fight the war and politicians should stay out of it."[lxi]

As a nation, a people and a society we must never allow ourselves to forget those who did not come home. They will die only when we no longer remember them and no longer honor their memory.

EPILOGUE II
Fragments of Memory
1966-1969

Fort Gordon, Georgia, 1966

<u>Drill Instructor (D.I.)</u>: "You 'best' run long and hard troop if you don't want to wind up a 'f _ _ _ _ ng recycle'."

<u>From Acclaimed Army Combat Trainer, Sergeant Morton</u>: "Now listen up, if the enemy sees you before you see the enemy...then <u>oop</u>, yo ass is gone."

<u>Squad Leader's Reply to every Complaint</u>: "As they say in Saigon, sorry about <u>that shit!</u>"

<u>Platoon Sergeant</u>: "If your belt buckle, your leather, your bunk and your weapon ain't standing tall, then you ain't no strak trooper. You are one sorry excuse for a human being."

<u>D.I.</u>: "You mean to tell me you reached the age of 22 years old without learning how to squat. Well, that's just pathetic." "Get down and start pushing up Georgia (pronounced Georgy) ...give me fifty... and yell them out like you got a set!"

"Yes drill sergeant."

"Heh troop you eat yet? No, well then go eat chow...but shave with dry sand first."

"You got peach fuzz on your face, you don't eat chow."

"Yes, Sir".

"Don't Sir me. I ain't no officer. I work for a living."

• Hand to Hand Combat Instructor:

Q: "Men, what is the spirit of the bayonet?" A: "To kill" (group response).

• <u>D.I.</u>: "If the enemy hits you with gas, you best get that mask on fast or your sorry ass is history...and you best be quick about stabbing yourself with that atropine surette...because I don't want to be the one who has to write your momma and your daddy to tell them their little boy ain't coming home."

"See men, I hate it when one of you gets wasted...It just makes too much paper work for me."

"Quit your g.d. milling around and stop playing grab ass."

<u>On a forced march</u>: "Take five and smoke 'em if you got 'em; and if you got 'em, give one to your buddy...when you're done, you best field strip that butt, or you can police the whole parade grounds after chow."

<u>Platoon Sergeant</u>: "Police the area men. If it ain't growing, pick it up."

<u>D.I.</u>: "Right face! No troop, your other right."

<u>Platoon Sergeant</u>: "The further up the line you go, the tougher it gets. And some of you ain't going to make it."

<u>Drill Instructor</u>: "What we want to teach you is to kill the enemy, to kill him before he kills you because there ain't nothing more pitiful and shameful than for you to get killed by something as dirty, as smelly and as lowdown as the enemy, as Charlie." (nickname for the Viet Cong)

• <u>Career Noncom</u>: "I'm good to go, to the 'Nam...just like I couldn't wait to get to Europe in WW 2 and to Korea."

"Why? Because the Army stateside is nothing but Mickey Mouse. The Nam is the big Green Valley."

<u>Drill Instructor</u>: "You got a chance of making it in the 'Nam son but if you're a college boy or from New York, you already have two strikes against you. The only thing they got in New York is queers and juvenile delinquents."

On Assignment, 1968

<u>Dave</u>: "Yeah the VC rocket went through the wall, over my bunk and missed my head by about a foot. My C.O. saw the hole in the wall

and said he was putting me in for an Army Commendation Medal. All I could think about was the bottle of Johnny Walker Red in my footlocker. I drank the whole thing that night."

Walt: "An old lifer, a Chief Warrant Officer, kept saying to me during Tet that it was worse than the Battle of the Bulge and kept praising me for being fearless in battle. Hell, I was just trying to keep busy and to survive. But the Chief gave us something to laugh about every time he described it as worse than the Battle of the Bulge. I guess he kept us from thinking about our predicament."

Paul: "Yeah, we ate in a good French restaurant on the outskirts of Saigon once a week...that is until we went there one day and it was nothing but a pile of rubble - A teenager, V.C. no doubt, on a motor bike with explosives strapped to his waist, drove through the entrance one day during meal time and blew it away, and everyone in it too."

Mike: (Reporting on the fate of our barracks - mates from A. I.T.[lxii]) Because of their M.O.S. they were living in a safe-house in the boonies, somewhere between Saigon and the Mekong Delta, when the VC came through during Tet. They never had a chance. They were all wasted."

Endnotes

i   The First Battle by Otto J. Lehrack (2006 Presidio Press), p. 45.

ii   Ibid.

iii   The First Battle, Ibid, p. 65.

iv   The First Battle, Ibid, p. 114.

v   Id.

vi   We were Soldiers Once...and Young, by Lt. Gen. Harold G. Moore (Ret.) and Joseph L. Galloway (Ballantine Books, Random House, 1992), p. 19.

vii   We were Soldiers, Once and Young, Ibid, p. 66.

viii Ibid, p. 68.

ix   Ibid, p. 69.

x   Ibid.

xi   Ibid, p. 168.

xii   Wikipedia - en.Wikipedia.org

xiii Eyewitness Vietnam by Donald L. Gilmore with D. M. Giangreco (Sterling Publishing Co., Inc., 2006).

xiv   Military Occupational Specialty.

xv   See Medal of Honor Citations, Vietnam and Gulf Wars.

xvi   American Valor, PBS biography of Drew D. Dix.

xvii American Valor, Ibid.

xviii See Medal of Honor Citations, Vietnam and Korea.

xix   Eyewitness Vietnam, Ibid at page 166.

xx   Ibid, p. 166.

xxi   Ibid, p. 167.

xxii Cpl. Dennis M. Mannion Remembers Hill 881s; www.hmmm-3 64.org./Mannion_d.

xxiii   Ibid.

xxiv   Ibid.

xxv   A Walk in the Clouds, Zollie Bean Pictures, 2004.

xxvi   Id.

xxvii   Lest We Forget by James Webb, Parade Magazine, May 27, 2001.

xxviii   Lest We Forget, Ibid.

xxix   Medal of Honor, One Man's Journey from Poverty and Prejudice by Roy P. Benavidez, First Brassey's Paperback Edition.

xxx   See U.S. Medal of Honor Citation, the source of some of the foregoing factual information.

xxxi   The Battle of Khe Gio Bridge by Don Wittenberger © 1999.

xxxii   Id.

xxxiii   Id.

xxxiv   When I was a Young Man, by Bob Kerrey (Harcourt, Inc., 2002) p. 104.

xxxv   When I was a Young Man, Ibid, p. 151.

xxxvi   When I was a Young Man, Ibid, p. 159.

xxxvii   Ibid, p. 178.

xxxviii   The New York Times Magazine, April 29, 2001, What Happened in Thanh Phong by Gregory L. Vistica, p. 53.

xxxix   When I was a Young Man, Ibid, p. 184.

xl   When I was a Young Man, Ibid, p. 184.

xli   N.Y. Times Magazine, Ibid.

xlii   N.Y. Times Magazine, Ibid, p. 66.

xliii   N.Y. Times Magazine, Ibid, p. 66.

xliv   Newsday, Team Backs Kerrey, 4/30/01, p. A3.

xlv   Albuquerque Tribune, November 4, 2002, Kate Nelson, Reporter.

xlvi   The New York Times, November 4, 2002, Richard Goldstein.

xlvii   The New York Times, Ibid.

xlviii   Id.

xlix   The New York Times, Ibid.

l   The New York Times, Ibid.

li   Albuquerque Tribune, Ibid.

lii   Albuquerque Tribune, Ibid.

liii   Albuquerque Tribune, Ibid.

liv   Id.

lv   Id.

lvi   The New York Times, Ibid.

lvii   Stolen Valor by B.G.. Burkett and Glenna Whitley (Vanity Press, Inc., Dallas, Texas, 1998), p. 13.

lviii   Id.

lix   Id.

lx   Stolen Valor, Ibid, p. 14.

lxi   Newsday, Generations of Honor, Vietnam, November 12, 2006, p. 46.

lxii   "A.I.T." - Advanced Individual Training.

Acknowledgments

I gratefully acknowledge Otto J. Lehrack's <u>The First Battle</u> and Lt. General Harold L. Moore and Joseph L. Galloway's <u>We Were Soldiers Once.. .and Young</u> as the sources of much of the factual information concerning <u>Operation Starlight</u> and <u>The Battle of Ia Drang Valley</u>, respectively. Acknowledgment is also made of B.G. Burkett and Glenna Whitley's <u>Stolen Valor</u> as the source of some of the material for the profile of Harry W. Horton, Jr.

Although not specifically chronicled in the text of this book, special mention should also be made of the thousands of members of the <u>United States Coast Guard</u> who served with distinction on vessels off the coast of Vietnam in the South China Sea. Their heroic rescues are the stuff of legend, and particular remembrance should be accorded to those men who gave their lives in that cause.

Acknowledgment is also made of the rich sources of historical and biographical data provided by Donald L. Gilmore and D.M. Giangreco in their book, <u>Eyewitness Vietnam</u>; by Roy P. Benavidez in his autobiography, <u>Medal of Honor, One Man's Journey from Poverty and Prejudice</u>; by Don Wittenberger in <u>The Battle of Khe Gio Bridge</u>, and by Bob Kerrey in <u>When I Was a Young Man</u>.

The reportorial skill and thoroughness of Gregory L. Vistica played prominently in the profile of Bob Kerrey. Mr. Vistica's article published in the <u>New York Times Magazine</u> on April 29, 2001, *What Happened in Thanh Phong,* was a font of relevant information.

I acknowledge with fondness and gratitude my comrades in arms during the time of the Vietnam War, who, although they certainly didn't know it then, provided me with rich texture for my effort to comprehend the Vietnam experience from the G.I.'s point of view. Particularly noteworthy is the anecdotal information provided to me by Vietnam Vets, Dave Holum, Paul Happy, John DeSmith and Walter Bailey during our conversations in 1968 and 1969.

Donald Farinacci

Finally, I wish to pay special thanks to Vietnam Veteran and former United States Air Force Officer William Christ for his perceptive introduction to <u>Last Full Measure of Devotion</u>.

Donald J. Farinacci

Made in the USA